Finnish-American Folklore

The Legend of St. Urho

Essays, Celebrations, Illustrations,
Grapes, and Grasshoppers

Compiled by Joanne Asala

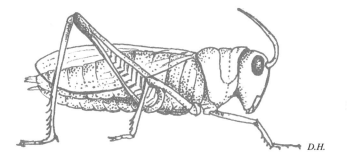

D.H.

"Canst thou make him afraid as the grasshopper?"
—Job 39:20

Penfield
Press

Dedication

For my father, Ronald Asala,
who taught me to take pride in my Finnish heritage.

Acknowledgments

Researching the legend of St. Urho has been one of my most enjoyable projects. I'd like to thank the many people who were of assistance, sharing their stories of past Urho celebrations; I'm particularly grateful to all those listed in this book with their essays or with their songs and quotes. I'd also like to thank Professor Michael Holmes, University of Utah, for permission to quote from his website on St. Urho, and for reading the completed manuscript; my mother Donna Asala; Timo Ryynanen of St. Urho's Pub in Helsinki, Finland; Bernhard Hillila, David Torrel, and especially Janice Laulainen — St. Urho's own historian.

Grasshopper illustrations by: Diane Heusinkveld, Michael Croes and
   David Fitzsimmons
Cover photography: John Johnson and Joan Liffring-Zug Bourret

Assistant Editors: Janice Laulainen, David Torrel and Bernhard Hillila
Associate Editors: Dwayne M. and Joan Liffring-Zug Bourret,
   Dorothy Crum, Miriam Canter and Georgia Heald

Cover Design: Deborah Walkoczy
Graphic Designer: M.A. Cook Design

Publisher's note: *The author and publisher have made every effort to track down the rightful copyright holders for several of the songs, poems, and excerpts included in this book. The very nature of folklore, however, often makes this task difficult, and true authorship is lost in the mists of time — even for a legend as young as the story of St. Urho.*

Introduction to Urhomania

"I once asked an Irish-Catholic priest (right from the old sod) about all this St. Urho's Day business, and he replied, 'With conditions as bad as they are in the world today, we need all the saints we can muster!'"
—Clarence Ivonen, editor
Mesabi Daily News
Virginia, Minnesota

March is a prime time for saints, not the least of which is Saint Urho, the Finnish-American hero created almost fifty years ago as a way for Finns to celebrate their ethnic heritage. As someone who is fully one-half Finn, I proudly don the colors of purple and Nile green for each March 16 celebration, and chant the ancient saint's curse, *"Heinäsirkka, heinäsirkka, mene täältä hiiteen!"* which translates, depending on whom you ask, as "Grasshopper, Grasshopper, go away /to heck/to hades/to the devil!" As with the festivities for that other celebrated March saint — whose name we will not mention here — everyone can take part in St. Urho's Day celebrations and drink purple beer, eat *feelia sour* (a sour milk pudding) and *mojakka* (fish stew), and exchange long underwear with their closest friends. But what is this? You've never heard of St. Urho? Ah, then let me tell you the story.

In the 1950s a small group of Finns decided to shake the throne of the Irish saint with the celebration of St. Urho's Day on March 16 — just one day before that March 17 celebration. Originating in the frosty land of Minnesota, thanks to the creativity of Richard Mattson, a Finnish-American department store manager, and Professor Sulo Havumaki of Bemidji State University, St. Urho is created and credited with having saved the Finnish grape harvest which was threatened by a plague of hungry grasshoppers. Legend has it that Urho, whose name means "hero" or "brave," raised his staff and bellowed the now famous Finnish phrase, "Grasshopper, grasshopper, go to hell!" The result? He rid Finland of the pesky critters and saved the wine-grape harvest.

Skeptics beware — it doesn't matter that there is no wine-grape crop in Finland nor has there ever been. And don't think to mention that Finland, like every other country in the world, is still plagued by hoppers. St. Urho's Day is officially recognized in all fifty states of the union and even has its adherents in Finland! Many Finns and Finnish-wannabes celebrate Urho's remarkable feat with parades, parties, and games of skill. Others re-enact Urho's miracle by repeating his famous command to the hoppers or reciting the "Ode to St. Urho." Still others will march through the streets of town, pitchforks in hand, ready to stab any hoppers that get in the way. You think we're crazy? Perhaps we are. But any culture who gave the world the sauna can't be all that bad.

—Joanne Asala

Joanne Asala is an author, editor and adventure traveler based in Illinois. She has written more than thirty books on folklore, fairy tales, and ethnic topics, including several for Penfield Press. Her father's family, whose original surname is Asiala, is 100 percent Finnish. Joanne is able to trace her Finnish ancestors back to 1490 — two years before Columbus landed in North America! The original family farm in Toholampi, Finland, has been occupied by the Asialas for more than 500 years.

David Fitzsimmons' drawing of a grasshopper from Joyful Nordic Humor. *David is a newspaper cartoonist in Tucson, Arizona, and is married to the Finnish-American niece of Esther and Bernhard Hillila. He illustrated the book* FinnFun *by Bernhard Hillila.*

Contents

continued

Tiss issa kuut puuk.
Eino tat iss my putter he iss sain tat tu.
Ten Eino he say tat pout time tey rites
ta puuk pout tat kuy, Urho.
                              —Toivo Töyrylä

The First St. Urho's Day

The following story comes from the May 25, 1956 edition of the Mesabi Daily News, *Virginia, Minnesota. It is the first known mention of St. Urho ever to be published.*

"If Richard L. Mattson, department store manager of Ketola's, thought his tall tales about 'Saint Urho' had not struck a responsive note last March 17, 1956, St. Patrick's Day, he had an opportunity to think otherwise yesterday, May 24.

Richard L. Mattson

"While the sons and daughters of Erin were paying their respects to St. Patrick, Mattson was loudly praising the feats of 'Saint Urho,' who, he claimed, had chased all the frogs out of Finland.

"Thursday afternoon, when employees of Ketola's Department Store went to the lounge, which is maintained for them in the basement of the store for their coffee breaks, they were greeted by a salute to Saint Urho's Day, designed particularly for Mattson's benefit.

"A hand-carved nutcracker, made in the shape of a native Filipino and to which had been affixed a miniature halo, was mounted on a mechanical hobby horse. Resting below him on the table was a huge, brilliantly green frog, symbolic of those from which Mattson said St. Urho had freed Finland.

"Across a mirror was a hand-lettered banner: *'Iloinen* St. Urho's *Päivä* — Happy St. Urho's Day,' but the piéce de résistance of the salute was a hand-lettered scroll containing the 'Ode to St. Urho,' written in Finglish dialect by an Irish girl."

Ode to Saint Urho
by Mrs. Gene McCavic
(written in "Finglish" dialect)

Ooksie Kooksie coolama vee
Saint Urho iss ta poy for me!
He sase out ta rogs so pig unt kreen
Prafest Finn I effer seen!

Some celeprate for Saint Pat unt hiss nakes
Putt Urho poyka got what it takes.
He got tall unt trong, from feelia sour
Unt ate culla mojakka effery hour.

That's why tat guy could soot tose rogs
What crew as pig as chack bine logs.
So let's giff a cheer in hower pest way
On May dwenny fort, Saint Urho's Day.

Author's note: *There is no way that Mrs. Gene McCavic, the Irish lass who wrote the "Ode to St. Urho," could have known her poem would become known the world over. Various versions of it are chanted with pride each St. Urho's Day.*

D.H.

In the beginning of the legend there were frogs....

St. Urho's Debut
by Richard L. Mattson

Richard Mattson, former manager of Ketola's Department Store, Virginia, Minnesota, is a pioneer of the Urho legend. In the following account, he fondly remembers the first St. Urho's Day celebration held in Virginia. This essay and facts about Richard Mattson, one of the men behind the saint, are adapted from Joyful Nordic Humor.

Winters are long and cold in Virginia, Minnesota, located on the Iron Range. Mrs. Gene McCavic, a co-worker at Ketola's Department Store, chided me that the Finns did not have saints like St. Patrick, so I told her the Irish aren't the only ones with great saints. She asked me to name one for the Finns.

So I fabricated a story and thought of St. Eero, St. Jussi, and St. Urho. Urho, a common Finnish name, had a more commanding sound. So I said, "We have St. Urho. To save the grape crop, he drove the poisonous frogs from Finland before the last Ice Age."

The women decided to have a St. Urho party in Ketola's coffee room. They made a cake with purple and green frosting. Mrs. McCavic wrote a poem in her "Finglish" dialect.

Clarence Ivonen of the *Mesabi Daily News* soon featured the birth of this new saint in, of all places, a department store. The folk legend of St. Urho grew; others embellished the original poem and wrote their own versions.

Through the years, I have given lectures on this long-neglected saint, explaining to rapt audiences that he was born of peasant stock on the Finnish-Swedish border. After showing promise in schools, he was given a scholarship to a Stockholm seminary, and studied in Paris under the humanist Catholic theologians.

When Urho returned to Finland, he was given a parish in a rural area. There he was constricted, feeling he had more to give. Since he knew the language, he was transferred to southern Finland, where farmers grow barley and oats. A small creek and bogs created an ideal breeding ground for poisonous frogs. When the oats and barley had tender shoots, the frogs amassed and crawled over the shoots, leaving the poison secreted from their skins. This had a devastating effect on the new young crops. The people appealed to the gods of *The Kalevala* (a Finnish epic) and then to the Christian God with no results. In desperation, they asked their new priest, good Father Urho, to help them.

After studying the problem and the height of a frog jump, Urho built a sluice high enough to contain the frogs by a meadow along the stream. They eventually went to a holding pond. Then the frogs were sailed to France in the holds of ships with ice to preserve them. Thanks to the Finns, this is how the French first acquired their taste for frog legs.

There is only one problem. Finland has never had a grape crop. While *The Kalevala*, the national Finnish epic poem, mentions poisonous toads, I thought frogs would be more appealing.

There is also a story about how Winston Churchill was inspired by St. Urho. While a young reporter for the *London Times*, Churchill covered Finland, its land and peoples. While in Samiland, also known as Lapland, he marveled at the beauty of the northland, and, upon leaving, noted the Sami people made a "V" sign as they were taught to do by St. Urho. Churchill's interpreter told him the fingers in a "V" meant "Peace to you." Later, during World War II, when he needed a rallying symbol in England, he remembered up with the "V" sign and made it a Victory sign.

Originally, St. Urho's Day was to be a May celebration, but everyone wanted to have the party in March as the Finnish answer to St. Patrick! The response became phenomenal — going nationwide within a few years with programs, parades, parties, greeting cards and buttons. I have heard there is a movement in the southwestern states to make St. Urho the patron saint of refrigeration, which makes it possible to ship fresh fruits and vegetables to the rest of the nation. Who knows when and where miracles will end?

A letter to the editor of the *Finnish-American Reporter* states, "Back in the days before he was a saint, Urho was known to occasionally lose his temper. One time, when he was dipping a fish net into a tank of lutefisk, the bottom of the net was eaten away by lye. In his anger, Urho hurled the net across the room, and it stuck in a crack in the wall. Still angry, he flung a piece of flat rye bread in the same direction. Much to his delight, the flatbread banged off the wall, went through the net, and rolled back to him. He decided to make a game of it, which he called 'Bread-kit Ball,' which naturally evolved into basketball."

As the legend grew, a Bemidji State University professor of psychology, Sulo Havumaki, in 1958, changed St. Urho's history from frogs to grasshoppers. And grasshoppers it has been ever since.

Columnist Jim Kloubuchar of the *Minneapolis Star* wrote that, "St. Patrick merely drove the snakes out of Ireland, working a shrewd trade-off with the future settlers of America, who took the snakes and residual rights to 'My Wild Irish Rose.' St. Urho had no such patsies. Working strictly on his own and without benefit of press agents or flit guns, St. Urho drove the grasshoppers out of Finland. He thus saved the Finnish grape crop, without which thousands of Swedes and Norwegians would have died of thirst."

Two statues of St. Urho were created with logs and chain saws at Menahga and Finland, Minnesota. The Menahga Urho is a thirteen-foot statue of the saint with a giant grasshopper impaled on a pitchfork. A spaghetti dinner reportedly honored the saint. Purple doughnuts made an appearance in New York Mills. Hugh Mellin of New York Mills, Minnesota, claimed to have found the saint's burial site nearby. Joseph Kyllonen, according to a newspaper account, is credited for the governors of every state proclaiming March 16 as St. Urho's Day.

A book published in Finland about Finns who live in other countries, *Ulkosuomalaisia (Outside Finns)*, featured St. Urho, the living legend. Ritva Paavolainen wrote the essay after we corresponded.

While in Finland in the late 1980s, I visited St. Urho's Pub, a workingman's bar close to the Parliament building. There were three silhouettes of monks in the front windows. I was astounded and continue to be amazed as St. Urho's Day is celebrated decades later at parties and festivities throughout America with people wearing green for grasshoppers and purple for grapes.

Richard Mattson, Mentor to the Saint

"A lot of saints and great men have been forgotten. Many saints have been condemned. I hope St. Urho will live on."

In 1956 Richard created his version of Saint Urho, a remarkable feat for a Minnesotan and a Lutheran Finn who is not a pope. Richard says, "I am proud of St. Urho; Finnish pride is like *sisu*. When they build a log cabin it is perfect. They keep fish nets repaired, and they bathe regularly in saunas. Bathing in Finland and Finnish America is a ritual. It is not just to get clean, although that comes with it." Born on July 4, 1913, Richard is a third-generation Finnish-American who grew up on the Iron Range of Minnesota. The Finnish family surname, Porspakka, was changed when Richard's grandfather worked as a fisherman on the Great Lakes and others called him Matt Mattson. Richard's father worked as an electrician for a sawmill, then opened a hardware store in Finn Town, and later became a partner of the Ketola Department Store in Virginia, Minnesota. Richard worked for his father and eventually managed the main floor of the Ketola Department Store for forty years.

Richard attributes a talent for performance and his love of a good time to his mother, Hannah. Participation in local theatrical and singing groups attest to a particular creativity that blossomed in a most unpredictable and unique fashion.

St. Urho's Pub in Helsinki

Richard Mattson, who popularized St. Urho, stands in front of St. Urho's Pub, Museokatu 10, Helsinki, Finland, in the 1980s. The pub celebrates the brave Finnish saint's day every March 16.

Urho Kekkonen was elected president of Finland in March 1956 — around the same year, Richard Mattson and Sulo Havumaki are credited with creating the legend of St. Urho. Many people believe that the popularity of this Finnish politician may have accelerated the spread of St. Urho's Day celebrations around the world. According to Mr. Timo Ryynänen, who works at St. Urho's, the pub was named after President Urho Kekkonen and "although we now celebrate March 16 in style, it's pure coincidence that you got this saint named Urho." Founded in 1973, St. Urho's Pub boasts a list of over eighty Finnish, English, German and Scottish ciders and beers. It consistently shows up on a list of the "Top Ten Pubs in Finland."

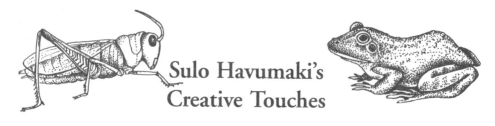

Sulo Havumaki's
Creative Touches

As is true with folklore the world over, legends are often adapted and embellished with many people contributing to the myth. Sulo Havumaki, a college professor at Bemidji State University in Minnesota, insisted that St. Urho chased the grasshoppers (not the frogs) out of Finland, and the legend has referred to grasshoppers ever since.

According to a number of people, Havumaki should receive credit for the creation of St. Urho. His daughter, Tana Havumaki, says her father celebrated St. Urho "long before anyone in any department store on any Iron Range had ever thought about it."

She continues: "In 1955 we were living in St. Paul, Minnesota, where dad was a psychologist for the city school district. We lived there only one year prior to moving to Bemidji. The majority of the population was Irish Catholic. In Finnish self defense and with lots of humor, he started St. Urho's Day using March 16 to steal a bit of glory from those St. Pat's revelers. I remember his coming home from work that day with a bouquet of purple carnations, received from staff in recognition of 'his holiday.'"

Dr. Havumaki's sister, Mrs. Elsie Mestnick of Gilbert, Minnesota, recently recalled that her brother even talked of St. Urho in high school. Dr. Havumaki deserves considerable credit for popularizing the saint. His version of the legend, in which he changed the frogs to grasshoppers, adorns the plaque of the St. Urho statue in Menahga, Minnesota.

Doris Havumaki stood in for her husband at the dedication of the statue, cracking a bottle of wine across Urho's foot. "Kind of a waste of a good bottle of wine," she is quoted as saying. According to daughter Tana, "I know my father would find all this extremely amusing. The point is that Finns everywhere now have a rallying day, and Dad would agree that this is what ultimately is important."

Photo by Allen Underm, The Enterprise, *Menahga*

1996 St. Urho Celebration, Menahga, Minnesota. King John Matthews and Queen Elsie Veit are shown with official crowns of grapes on their hats. The Statue of St. Urho, in the background, features a grasshopper, symbolic of the hoppers the saint drove out of Finland. The statue is located on Highway 71 which passes through Menahga. In 1975 a contest was held for the purpose of creating a likeness of Urho. Rita Seppala was the winner, and the task of carving the statue eventually fell to chain-saw artist Jerry Ward. Assisting Ward was local artisan Elmer Lalli. When parts of the original wooden statue rotted, a fiberglass copy was installed.

The Legend of St. Urho
by Sulo Havumaki

The text of Professor Havumaki's version of the legend is found on the plaque at the base of the statue in Menahga, Minnesota.

One of the lesser known, but extraordinary legends of ages past, is the legend of St. Urho — patron saint of the Finnish vineyard workers.

Before the last glacial period, wild grapes grew with abundance in the area now known as Finland. Archeologists have uncovered evidence of this scratched on the thigh bones of the giant bears that once roamed northern Europe. The wild grapes were threatened by a plague of grasshoppers until St. Urho banished the lot of them with a few selected Finnish words.

In memory of this impressive demonstration of the Finnish language, Finnish people celebrate on March 16, the day before St. Patrick's Day. It tends to serve as a reminder that St. Pat's Day is just around the corner and is thus celebrated by squares at sunrise on March 16. Finnish women and children, dressed in royal purple and Nile green, gather around the shores of many lakes in Finland and chant what St. Urho chanted many years ago: *"Heinäsirkka, heinäsirkka, mene täältä hiiteen!"* (Translated: "Grasshopper, Grasshopper, go away!")

Adult male (people not grasshoppers) dressed in green costumes gather on the hills overlooking the lakes, listen to the chant and then kicking out like grasshoppers, they slowly disappear to change costumes from green to purple. The celebration ends with singing and dancing polkas and schottisches and drinking grape juice, though these activities may occur in varying sequences.

Color for the day is royal purple and Nile green.

Snapshots from Historic St. Urho Days

Joseph Kyllonen, former National Director of St. Urho's Day, was instrumental in getting the governors of all fifty states to proclaim March 16th a holiday in honor of the saint. Kyllonen's license plates advertised the fact that Minnesota is not just the Land of 10,000 Lakes.

President Urho Kekkonen of Finland is kissed in 1976 by Janice Laulainen, St. Urho "historian" of Minneapolis.

Janice Laulainen places a St. Urho's Day pin on Governor Wendell Anderson in 1975.

Official Recognition!

In 1975, Minnesota Governor Wendell Anderson officially proclaimed March 16 "for all years to come" as St. Urho's Day. In 1977, Governor Rudy Perpich made the same proclamation in Finnish.

WHEREAS: a significant number of residents of Minnesota are of Finnish descent; and

WHEREAS: this distinguished group of citizens has contributed substantially in many ways to the pioneer settlement and subsequent development of the great state of Minnesota; and

WHEREAS: this ethnic group through the years has continually honored their heritage with great fortitude and an enviable sense of humor as recipients of numerous amusing but questionable and unlikely tales of Finnish endeavor; and

WHEREAS: descendants of this noteworthy nationality have adopted the renowned St. Urho as the Patron Saint of Finnish people in commemoration of his great deed, saving the grape crop in Finland by driving the grasshoppers out of that country with the now famous words, *Heinäsirkka, heinäsirkka, mene täältä hiiteen*;

NOW, THEREFORE, I, Wendell R. Anderson, Governor of Minnesota, do hereby proclaim March 16th, 1975, and March 16 of all the years to come as

St. Urho's Day

In Minnesota to be celebrated accordingly by all people of Finnish descent and friends.

IN WITNESS WHEREOF I have hereunto set my hand and caused the Great Seal of the State of Minnesota to be affixed at the State Capitol this twelfth day of March in the year of our Lord one thousand nine hundred and seventy-five and of the State, the one hundred and seventeenth.

Wendell R. Anderson, Governor

St. Urho:
A Patron Saint for the New World Finns
by Borje Vähämäki

The following essay is adapted from an address Professor Vähämäki, Director of Finnish Studies, University of Toronto, Ontario, Canada, made at the Toronto Suomi Lion's Club in 1993. He explores the cultural origins of St. Urho and the saint's place in modern folklore.

Introduction

On March 16 of each year, hoards of Finns and other good people in the United States, Finland, and Canada — perhaps even Sweden, Australia, and Brazil — celebrate St. Urho's Day. While living in Minnesota between 1975 and 1989, I became friends with many followers and scholars of St. Urho. Clarence Ivonen has recorded in his *Mesabi Daily News* several St. Urho celebrations, including the very first one held in Virginia, Minnesota. Leo Keskinen, who ran a Finnish radio station in Grand Rapids, Minnesota, was a pioneer in collecting documents and material on the St. Urho celebration. I have also consulted the writings of my friends Hannele Jönsson-Korhola, Matti Kaups, and Don Wirtanen in preparation for this address.

Before I elaborate on the central facts, the ritual texts, the function and the multitude of manifestations of the St. Urho myth, I'd like to say a few words on its age.

We know that most world mythologies of dignity and distinction date back to the distant past, often prehistoric times. We also know quite well that one of the central cultural values among the Finnish people is reverence for age. To the Finns, old age implies — in fact equals — wisdom. We need only recall what happens to the young upstart shaman Joukahainen in *The Kalevala* when he challenges Väinämöinen, the cultural hero and the eternal sage, to a contest of wits. It is quite clear that when Joukahainen is magically sung into a marsh, it is not a consequence of his shortcomings in knowledge, but his lack of reverence for Väinämöinen's old age.

The comparatively young age of the St. Urho myth, which in the form we know it dates back to 1956, is counterbalanced by the supposed ancient heroic deeds of the saint. According to tradition, Urho chased the grasshoppers out of Finland thousands of years ago. This address will introduce this decades-old myth of more than 3,000 years of age — a tale that may even date back to pre-Ice Age Finland!

While the deeds of St. Urho date way back in time, the actual written documents of this myth have been traced down to March 16, 1956, and/or May 24, 1956. It is not known whether these documents were written a.m. or p.m. of the dates indicated above, but it has been convincingly put forward that it must have occurred during the hours of darkness when spiritual sensitivities are heightened.

Preamble

Before we analyze further the validity of these two somewhat conflicting origins, I would like to present the conditions and context of St. Urho's heroism. This is how the story goes (Hannele Jönsson-Korhola):

Many millennia ago in the Old World there grew naturally and in abundance grapes of the greatest quality. Archeological finds show this engraved in thighbones of giant bears which roamed Northern Europe in primordial times.

One year an enormous flock of grasshoppers arrived from the east, threatening the entire grape crop. That is when St. Urho demonstrated the unique power of the Finnish language by driving the grasshoppers out of Finland with a few select words.

It is in commemoration of this impressive performance by the Patron Saint of the Finns that St. Urho's Day is celebrated on the sixteenth day of each March. By coincidence, this event is just one day before St. Patrick's Day, which honors another heroic saint. (There is no evidence to suggest that a relationship exists between the saints themselves, such as the idle notion that the snakes St. Patrick chased out of Ireland ate the grasshoppers that St. Urho chased into the sea.)

Dressed in royal purple (the color of the juicy grapes) and in Nile green, engaging in ceremonial behavior conspicuously ritual in nature, the men, women, and children dance, hop and chant repeatedly the mighty words of St. Urho:

"Heinäsirkka, heinäsirkka, mene täältä hiiteen!"

It goes without saying that drinking the juice of grapes is an elemental part of the celebration.

Triumphant

Problems With The Myth: Frogs or Grasshoppers?

Flattened

The study of the myth of St. Urho is greatly facilitated by the fact that there are two myth texts extant. The largely similar versions of "Ode to St. Urho," both having originated in Minnesota, are retained in historic archives.

Ode to St. Urho #1
Ooksie kooksie coolama vee
Santia Urho is ta poy for me!
He sase out ta hoppers as pig as birds.
Neffer perfoor haff I hurd does words!
He reely told does pugs of kreen
Prafest Finn I effer seen.
Some celeprate for St. Pat unt hiss nakes
Putt Urho poyka got vat it takes.
He got tall an´ trong from feelia sour
Unt ate culla mojakka effery hour.
Tat's why dat guy could sase dose peetles
Vat krew as thick as chack bine needles.
So let's give a cheer in hower pest vay
On the sixteenth of March, St. Urho's Tay.

An older version of twelve lines, while very similar, displays two significant differences: 1) St. Urho chased out frogs not grasshoppers, and 2) St. Urho's Day is on May 24 rather than March 16. The text follows:

Ode to St. Urho #2
Ooksie kooksie coolama vee
Santia Urho iss ta poy for me!
He sases out ta rogs so pig unt kreen
Prafest Finn I effer seen!
Some celeprate for St. Pat unt hiss nakes
Putt Urho poyka got what it takes.
He got tall unt trong from feelia sour.
Unt ate culla mojakka effery hour.
Tat's why tat guy could soote tose rogs
What crew as pig as chack bine logs.
So let's giff a cheer in hower pest way
On May tvenny fort, Saint Urho's Tay.

When we take a close look at these two versions of the "Ode to St. Urho," we find that they clearly represent the genre of the heroic poem. The description of his brave deeds, the revelation of the source of his extraordinary powers, and the expression of praise and adoration — ending with an encouragement for the people to celebrate Urho — are hallmarks of an epic poem.

There are two other prominent phenomena which require comment. The first is the language. There is a unique sound structure to the ode, a distinct dialect of the English language as spoken by Finnish immigrants and their descendants.

The first line "Ooksie kooksie coolama vee" stands for the Finnish words "*yksi, kaksi, kolme* and *viis*" — in English, "one, two, three, and five." They have been absorbed into the English language, in this case passing for English words.

If you are familiar with the Finnish phonetic system, you may know that several English sounds or sound combinations are unknown in Finnish, such as **b**, **d**, **f**, **g**, **th**, **sh**, and **ch**. Also, it is important to remember that Finnish normally does not have consonant clusters at the beginning of words. The English words chase, snakes, and strong might be unpronouncible to a native Finn, and come out something like sase, nakes, trong, or rong.

In the case of "Ode to St. Urho," it has not been reliably determined whether the language of the ode represents how others, such as the Irish, would mockingly imitate Finns' pronunciation of English or whether the language rendition represents the wholesome, healthy sense of humor found among the Finns and their descendants. Personally — and seriously, I might add — I lean toward the good Finnish humor theory. Not only does the imagery (*kalamojakka, viiliä, ta poy for me,* etc.) reflect Finnish "insider" humor, but there was already a veritable tradition of popular "Finglish" literature in the 1950s. I'll mention only Hap Puotinen's Finglish adaptations of Shakespeare, the Brothers Grimm, etc. Here is "No Vhite" from *Finglish Fables,* 1969. It is a clear illustration of the literature typical of the era.

No Vhite
(Finglish)
Vas Rinsess vun tine long ako,
An No Vhite vas her name;
Kviin Mudder tet long tine an so
Nuu Kviin for King tere came.
Tiss Kviin vas lil pit kine-a kiut
Put elsevise chust a vits,
Tat mirrol on ta vall sii put
An alvays asken it,
"Juu mirrol, mirrol, on tat vall
Chust vas tat mostest kiut for all?
Tont nevermine, tats mii!"

Grasshopper queen in mirror

(English)
There was once a Princess long ago,
And Snow White was her name;
The Queen Mother had died a long time ago

A new Queen there came for the King.
The Queen was quite good looking
But otherwise she was just a witch.
She put a mirror on the wall,
And always kept asking it:
"Mirror, mirror, on the wall
just tell me honestly!
Who is the fairest of them all?
Never mind, that's me!"

The second major difference between the versions is what Urho actually chased out of Finland. In Version One, it was grasshoppers; in Version Two, it was frogs. (It should be brought to our attention that all subsequent transcriptions and publications refer only to the grasshopper.) It has been convincingly shown by Ritva Paavolainen, in an article from 1981, that the frog version was construed consciously, but with elements of arbitrary coincidence.

This happened in Virginia, Minnesota, in 1956. Mr. Richard L. Mattson, department manager at the Ketola Department Store, felt that his stories of St. Urho, told on St. Patrick's Day, did not receive the attention and respect they deserved. To console him, his personnel decided to launch a St. Urho's Day that spring of 1956. They gathered in the employee lounge, which they had decorated with many details. The centerpiece was a giant green plastic frog from the toy department to represent the frogs from which St. Urho liberated Finland. (Inventory lists suggest that there were no grasshopper figures in stock.) There was also a note to Richard from an Irish employee thanking him for telling his people about this superman.

However, all subsequent citings make reference only to grasshoppers, as does the first version of the "Ode" which I quoted above.

This version also mentions grapes for the first time. It was initiated by psychology professor Sulo Havumaki of St. Paul, who moved to Bemidji in 1956. Soon the St. Urho paraphernalia were particular enough: the grasshoppers and grapes, the colors green and purple respectively, have become the standard.

St. Urho vs. St. Patrick

Many details of the "Ode" lead us to examine the legend more closely. Of particular interest is the relationship between the St. Urho legend and the St. Patrick tradition, and correspondingly between the Finns and the Irish, or more precisely between Finnish and Irish immigrants to North America. We have already pointed to a number of factors common to modern St. Urho and St. Patrick celebrations:

- Patron saints chasing undesirable, evil creatures out of their respective lands.
- The colors are shared: green and purple.
- The snakes allegedly ate the grasshoppers which had been chased out of Finland.
- The "Ode to St. Urho" mentions explicitly "some celebrate for St. Pat unt hiss nakes."
- The dates March 16 and 17 allow both groups' celebration by squares.
- Before 1956 St. Urho's tales were told mostly on St. Patrick's Day, at least in Virginia, Minnesota.
- The parade traditions are similar.

It is quite possible that Matti Kaups is correct when he writes (*Finnish Americana*, 1986): ". . . it seems that Finnish ancestry, exposure to the legend of St. Patrick, and residence in the land of such giants as Paul Bunyan and Babe, influenced the inner thoughts and motivated men to perpetuate the anachronistic farce of St. Urho. . . . Some have suggested that the alleged protracted animosity between the Irish and the Finns in the copper and iron mines of the Lake

Superior region led to the formation of the legend of St. Urho . . . an expression of one-upmanship on the part of the Finns over their fiercest rivals in the work place. Granted, there is an element of ethnic chauvinism in the legend . . . but there is no evidence whatsoever to support the one-upmanship thesis. And there are other predicaments around. . . ."

Such were the musings of Professor Kaups of Duluth, Minnesota. On a somewhat more serious note, I believe the Finnish-Irish arch rivalry and hostility is substantial, though deeply buried, as a background. Perhaps the good-naturedness of the St. Urho legend's modeling after the St. Patrick legend, points to improved, healed, inter-ethnic relations between the two groups. Occasionally, however, Irish "conservationists" heckle St. Urho's Day parades, protesting the slaughter of grasshoppers.

Other Questions of Origin or Why the Name Urho?

The name displays three properties of explanatory import:
- Urho in English translation means "hero" and, therefore, a most appropriate name.
- It also has phonetic likeness, particularly in its vowels, to Ukko, the supreme god in the national epic *The Kalevala*.
- More significant, perhaps, is the presence of the heroic, virile consonant **r**, **rrr**. Mr. Mattson confesses in a letter: "I tested out different Finnish names . . . St. Eino, St. Jussi, St. Eero . . . , but Urho had a more commanding sound." Leo Keskinen also believes Urho was chosen to allow Finns the opportunity to roll the **r** "in the typical Finnish fashion."

We must also recall the fact that in March, 1956, i.e., the month the "Ode" originated, Urho Kaleva Kekkonen became president of Finland. Whether the choice of the name Urho had anything to do in the beginning with Urho Kekkonen is shrouded in mist. The legend lay dormant for about a decade in the 1960s. Its revival in the early 1970s is entirely consistent with Urho Kekkonen's increasing prominence in status and stature in the eyes of Finnish Americans. Kekkonen visited the United States in 1961 and in 1976, and Finnish Americans and Finnish Canadians traveled in unprecedented numbers to Finland, and during each time, Urho Kekkonen was the president (1956-1981).

The Role of Psychology

The fact that "Founding Father" Number One, Sulo Havumaki, was a professor of psychology is not without relevance. In fact, it is also assumed that Richard Mattson possessed special psychological insights. We can safely conclude that the formulation, contents and timing of the St. Urho myth was psychologically most felicitous. I would like, however, to concur with Matti Kaups's suggestion that the legend awaits serious inquiry by professional psychologists, preferably experts trained in the art of Freudian psychoanalysis.

The Neutral Ideology Theory

For almost a century, Finnish immigrants and their descendants in North America were divided into Church Finns and Workers' Hall Finns. St. Urho's origin is really not to be attributed to either camp; in fact, these groups have "nominated" their own candidates for sainthood. Pastor Olaf Rankinen has suggested that it would have been more appropriate to celebrate another patron saint of Finland, St. Henry (Pyhä Henrikki), who in the twelfth century preached to the Finnish people. (Later, Henry was murdered by a soldier he had excommunicated.) Some other groups, including the Knights and Ladies of Kalevala, have alluded that Väinämöinen or Ilmarinen, heroes from the epic *Kalevala,* would have been more appropriate objects of celebration.

It is generally considered important that the legend of St. Urho survived and continued to grow because it offered a fresh, ideologically neutral and sufficiently distant primordial hero that could unite and inspire the Finns in North America and their descendants in their quest for expression and manifestation of their cultural bonding.

Let me try to give you an idea of the penetrations of this young legend into mainstream North America. Every single one of the USA's fifty states celebrates March 16 as St. Urho's Day. Many cities in Finland — sister cities or friendship cities to a U.S. counterpart — celebrate St. Urho. There are St. Urho Day parades in Minnesota, Wisconsin, and Michigan, as well as California and Pennsylvania. Here in Ontario, particularly in Thunder Bay and Sudbury, we have adopted the St. Urho tradition. It is observed also in Australia, Brazil, and Sweden — just to name a few countries.

A recent St. Urho's celebration in Thunder Bay featured The Finnish Men's Choir: OTAVA. According to choir member Pentti Junni, the typical St. Urho's Day is celebrated by the Finns of Thunder Bay in the following way:

The Saturday closest to March 16 is declared St. Urho's Day. At 2 p.m., a St. Urho's parade is held, although just a short few blocks, ending up at the Finlandia Hall. The paraders dress in something green and/or purple; they wear some St. Urho paraphernalia such as a grasshopper, grape clusters, pins and buttons, and carry rakes, hay forks or other farm implements. Some prominent member of the Finnish community plays the role of St. Urho himself clad in appropriate attire. At times even the mayor marches in the parade. Paraders will typically carry signs championing their pet social causes or with references to St. Urho's heroics. Every now and then the parade will stop for loud chants in unison of the mighty words of St. Urho, *"Heinäsirkka, heinäsirkka, mene täältä hiiteen!"*

At the end of the parade at Finlandia Hall, there will be light programs for about two hours. A central theme is to eat — just as St. Urho himself — *kalamojakka*, which on this special day is served in abundance. In the evening everybody gathers again for the St. Urho's dance, once again with dress and decor employing green, purple, grasshoppers and grapes, as well as variations and metamorphoses of these.

St. Urho Hops the Border

Croes

Grasshoppers dancing the tango, a Finnish favorite since 1913. The New World Finn *newspaper in 2001 reported that Buenos Aires politicians "suggest that their city and Seinäjoki, Finland be regarded as the tango capitals of the world."*

Occasionally some Irish St. Patrick celebrators will crash the party, but so will St. Urhonians in turn on St. Patrick's Day. All is in good humor. In fact, one year on St. Urho's Day the Irish hung a large banner in the city saying, "St. Patrick is #1." But the Finns, upon discovering this, quickly attached a humble subscript, "After St. Urho."

St. Urho and Commercialism

Some say that the St. Urho tradition survives because it is heavily commercialized. People and organizations, including Lions Clubs, sell St. Urho pins and buttons, tee shirts, postcards, caps, beer mugs, Finnish "donut seeds," and Urho burgers. They arrange golf tournaments (often on ice), dances, and suppers. Whether it is the commercialism that keeps the legend alive or whether it is the dynamic tradition that generates commercial by-products, remains yet to be determined.

Thoughts on the Power
of St. Urho's Words

While many sources refer to the power of the Finnish language itself, *"Heinäsirkka, heinäsirkka, mene täältä hiiteen!,"* I wish to draw your attention to the parallels with the power of the word in *The Kalevala*. That power is magic power and the source of the magic power lies in the shamanistic nature religion which the St. Urho myth shares with *The Kalevala*. In light of this, St. Urho apparently was a powerful and skilled shaman who was able to communicate with and exert power over the spirits of the natural beings. *"Heinäsirkka, heinäsirkka . . ."* is a charm in the best Kalevalaic tradition.

North American Origins

St. Urho is the patron saint of the Finnish Americans and Finnish Canadians. Statues of him that have been erected in Minnesota, show hay forks and locusts reminiscent of midwestern farm life in North America. There are many other American influences which prove the North American roots of this legend. May the beautiful arrangement of the "Ode to St. Urho" by professor Elmer Mattila of Minneapolis, Minnesota, to the melody of Davy Crockett, serve to illustrate this final point.

Elmer Mattila's Ode to St. Urho

He sase out ta hoppers as pig as birds.

Neffer peefor haff I hurd dose words!
He reely told dose pugs of kreen
Braffest Finn tat I effer seen.

Heinä, heinäsirkka, mene täältä hiiteen!
Heinä, heinäsirkka, mene täältä hiiteen!

Some celebrates for St. Pat unt hiss nakes
Put Urho poyka got what it takes.
He got tall und trong from feelia sour
Unt ate culla mojakka effery hour.

Urho Savumaki, Urho is ta poy for me.
Urho Savumaki, Urho is ta poy for me.

Tat's why dat guy culd sase dose peetles
what krew as thick as chack bine needles.
So let's give a cheer in hower pest way
On the sixteenth of March, St. Urho's Tay!

Urho Savumaki! Urho is ta poy for me!
Heinä, heinäsirkka, mene täältä hiiteen.

Some Last Words

I wish to conclude with a comment on St. Urho's last name Savumaki in Mattila's arrangement. The explanation offered by Mr. Mattila is that Savumaki is Urho's last name; he lives at the top of a volcanic mountain which is eternally shrouded in smoke. Savumaki means "smoke hill." Another hypothesis has been put forward that the name is related to the first father of the "Ode," Professor Sulo Havumaki, which with some mix-up in the letter could easily have become Savumaki.

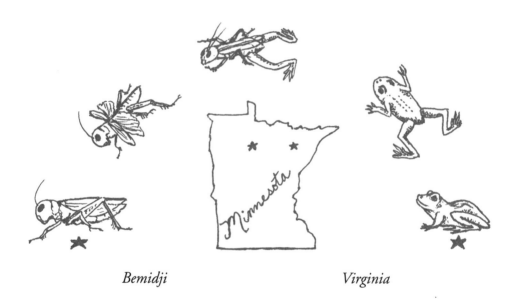

Bemidji   Virginia

Hoppers triumph over frogs in this illustration of St. Urho's folklore by Diane Heusinkveld.

A Bit of History

by Kauno Sihvonen

Each year Kauno Sihvonen and his wife Martha help in hosting a St. Urho's Day Banquet for "All Finns, Part Finns, Those Married to Finns, and All Friends of Finns." The following address was presented in Reno, Nevada, 1998. It presents a glimpse of the Finnish character.

Welcome to the seventeenth St. Urho's Day celebration to be held in Reno. It all started in 1981 when Niilo Hyytinen and a few Finnish friends decided to meet for lunch in a bar. Surprisingly the idea caught on, and here we are. St. Urho was unknown to me in the early 80s, but we were ready to honor that ancient, mystical Finn. You all know the story. When hoards of grasshoppers threatened to destroy the wild grapevines that covered Finland, a great hero named Urho came forth and with the terrifying words, *"Heinäsirkka, heinäsirkka, mene täältä hiiteen!"* he banished the creatures forever.

Oh, that was exciting history. But after a little thought, I began to wonder. Grapes covering Finland? Grasshoppers? And those magic words translated into "Grasshopper, Grasshopper, go to the devil's place." Investigating further exposed the hoax. It seems that a group of Finns in Minnesota, suffering from a long winter and envious of the Irish St. Patrick's Day that was coming up, decided to have their own celebration. So Urho, Finnish for hero or brave, was invented. Of course, he had to be a saint, too. Grapes and grasshoppers were added. And is was no coincidence that St. Urho's Day was to be celebrated one day before Patrick's.

The only reason it is not a national holiday is due to the modest, independent quiet nature of the Finns.

Let's explore these Finns a bit more — they are a Finno-Ugrian people who migrated from the Ural Mountains of Russia about 6,000 years ago. Eventually they settled north of the Baltic Sea in a land covered with forests, lakes, and rocks. It became known as

Suomi. It is interesting that *suo* means swamp. They lived as a tribal people without a central government or a written language, but these Finns became skilled fishermen, hunters, and boat builders, and they were expert at clearing land for farming.

In 1225, their more sophisticated neighbor, Sweden, decided to expand eastward, and so Finland was incorporated into its kingdom. For the next 600 years, Finns became second-class Swedes, almost losing their language skills. Then in the early 1800s, Finland was lost to Russia in a twenty-year war. Then the Russians tried to impose their government and language on the Finns. This created a great nationalistic movement to make the Finns more proud of their heritage and language. It was helped greatly by publication of *The Kalevala,* an epic foundation of Finnish identity.

Finnish is a beautiful language, but is one of the world's most difficult to learn. Sure, I could teach any of you to read Finnish in a few weeks. That's because their alphabet looks familiar and each letter always has the same sound. The **A** is always **A**, the **E** is **E**, **R** is **R**, **Y** is **Y**. Isn't that easy? But to understand the exact meaning of a word might take a lifetime of study. Finnish is an expressive language with great sensitivity to minute sound variations. Different words describe the wind blowing through pine trees and birches. There are over 700 words to describe degrees of inebriation! Finns love to drink! Now here's a tip for pronouncing Urho. Just think of gardening. Say, "Where's your hoe?" Get it? St. Your Hoe.

Now, here are a few facts about Finns that I've discovered. Finland has never fought a war to gain territory, but it has fought Russia forty-seven times — and lost every time. That's called *sisu,* a Finnish trait of stubbornness or determination.

Most of the great Viking ships were built by the Finnish craftsmen who traveled to Norway each summer. And you can bet that more than one pulled oars to Greenland and America.

In the years 1638 to 1655, the colony of New Sweden flourished at the mouth of the Delaware River in America.

Niilo Hyytinen, organizer of Reno's St. Urho celebration, wore the traditional symbols of purple grapes and a green grasshopper on his white sweatshirt.

Of the 2,000 inhabitants, most were Finns. The Swedes weren't dumb enough to leave the comforts of home, but the Finns were at home in the forest environment with the wild animals and the farming hardships. From this base, the Finns were on friendly terms with the natives and explored all the way to the Rocky Mountains. All this before the other colonists dared to venture a day's ride from home. And, not surprisingly, the Finns introduced log cabin building, the woodsman's axe, and cut-and-burn land clearing. This was just everyday life in Finland.

Of course, we know from our history that John Morton was the man whose vote broke the deadlock on independence for the thirteen colonies in 1776. What you may not know is that his ancestors came from Rautalampi, Finland, and the name evolved from Murtonen to Mortonen to Morton — but he was a Finn.

Big immigrations in the late 1800s brought many Finns to this country. With a lot of choice of land available, where did they settle? Maine, Minnesota, Michigan. Like in the home country, they wanted forests, lakes, rocky soil, and cold winters. And it was in this rugged land that the brave, hardy, proud and very independent Finns settled — and where a saint was born.

Battle of the Saints
by Sandy Hautanen

All four of Sandy's grandparents came to America from Finland. Her parents, Olavi S. Hautanen and Tuulikki Eleanora Jonhunen, spoke Finnish before they learned to speak English, and grew up together in the Finnish community in Buffalo, New York. This piece was originally published in the August 1996 issue of The Finnish-American Reporter *as "A Finnish-American in Boston." From* The Finnish-American Reporter. *Reprinted with permission.*

I celebrate St. Urho's Day in Boston. It isn't easy.

Being Finnish in Boston, first and foremost, means that no one will ever understand your last name. "It's Hautanen," I say patiently, and then I spell it. "All four of my grandparents came from Finland."

"Houghton?" asks the typical Bostonian, now confused. "You're not Irish?" "No," I say, with a forced smile. "I'm Finnish."

Month of March sign at Bergquist Imports, Inc., Cloquet, Minnesota

"The Vikings invaded Ireland," the Bostonian dimly recalls.

"And the Irish got scared and ran away," I say, now smiling hard, "to Boston."

(Well, I never really say this....I dislike physical violence, particularly when I'm having this discussion in an Irish pub in Boston on March 16th, the day before St. Patrick's Day, surrounded by locals who've had a few too many pints of Guinness. But it's true.)

If you say "Finn" in Boston, no one thinks of Finland. In Boston, the Finns live next door to the Kellys or are the Kennedys' cousins — "You know, Brendan Finn and his lovely wife Bridget. A fine couple."

According to Brian (yes, he's Irish) in my office, there are so many Irishmen in Boston that if you yell, "Hey, Sully!" at a Boston College football game, half the crowd will look up to see who's calling their name. But if you yell, "Hey, Hautanen!" people will probably think you're choking, grab you from behind and start doing the Heimlich maneuver. This would never happen in Duluth.

As every good Finnish American knows, March 16th is the day to honor the sainted Lutheran who threw the grasshoppers (or frogs, or whatever) off the wine grapes in Finland; we proudly wear purple for the wine grapes and green for the grasshoppers (or whatever) and raise our wineglasses to shouts of

or some other multi-voweled Finnish salute that means, "Grasshoppers (or whatever) go away so we can party!" (I should add that by wearing at least some green, no matter what the reason, you should survive if you do this on March 16th in Boston Common.) I believe such sacred customs should be faithfully observed.

I've read that in civilized cultures — like in Duluth — there are bold Knights of St. Urho who march through the late-winter slush in parades, and make ice sculptures to honor our hero. But alas, not in Boston.

March 16th in this corner of New England is simply the day before March 17th, the day of "The Parade" in South Boston. "The Parade" has something to do with leprechauns and green beer and a Catholic saint who took time off from converting the heathen

Irish to throw snakes off some sheep — or something like that. (What a stupid reason for a parade!) For years, "The Parade" has been run by a man named Wacko Hurley — really. "Wacko" and his fellow Hibernians take their parade very seriously. Parade-goers dress all in green (but Celtics shirts are okay, too). They have shamrocks drawn on their faces and wear silly green hats on their heads, and everyone speaks with an Irish/Boston brogue. Later they go to nearby pubs to quaff a few pints, hear some Irish music, and dance an Irish jig (most often while waiting in line for the loo). To me, it all seems so artificial, unlike our own solemn ethnic festivities.

I discovered St. Urho's Day several years ago in Washington, D.C., at a party on March 16th in a hardworking Minnesota congressman's office. Since then, in addition to honoring my Finnish roots by drinking Finlandia vodka out of Iittala glassware, I have made it my mission to spread the word about St. Urho. This usually means crashing St. Patrick's Day parties, a dangerous but most satisfying annual adventure.

My greatest success was at Ed's party in Newport, Rhode Island. When I arrived in the late afternoon, Ed and his friends had been drinking since lunch. So they didn't much mind when I put out purple grapes, Finn Crisp, Finlandia cheese, Marimekko napkins, and a number of bottles of wine, and then started pinning "Go St. Urho" buttons on the woozy guests. Later on, even Ed was lustily shouting, "Grasshoppers, go away!" — but only after I let him wear my special St. Urho's Day baseball cap with the big green plastic grasshopper sitting on top. It was a good day.

My worst day was at the Shannons' house, where I proudly brought along *karpalopuuro* to share with the crowd. Carefully following my mother's recipe, I had blended just the right amount of cranberry juice into Cream of Wheat, letting the porridge simmer on the stove. At the party, one of the ten Shannon kids warily eyed the bowl of what, I must admit, did look a little like gloppy pink wallpaper paste. She finally licked some *karpalopuuro* off a spoon. Grimacing politely, she said, "You Finns must be wicked brave to eat this stuff." Raising my eyebrows under my special grasshopper base-ball cap, I then tried some myself. Big mistake. I'd forgotten to add the sugar. I left that party early, but I'd learned a valuable lesson: just bring lots of wine.

I vow to continue my quest to spread the fame of St. Urho here in Boston. My next mission is to teach the fellow I'm dating how to pronounce my last name. Since he's a self-described "Mick" who went to Holy Cross, it won't be easy. But with the help of St. Urho, it just might be possible. And, if he catches on quickly, I might let him try on my baseball cap, too.

D.H.

Bug vs. Grasshopper

David Nohrenberg, who calls himself St. Urho's "Humple Serwent," drove his homemade "Bug" through the streets of Menahga with an 8-foot-long grasshopper in tow. Sadly, the grasshopper made a pass at the "Bug's" driveshaft during the town's St. Urho Day parade and got all tangled up. "Eventually," says Nohrenberg, "we'll have to adorn an 8-foot pine box with grapes and conduct a little farewell service." Menahga has had a Urho celebration for more than thirty years. "We have little choice," Nohrenberg adds, "we're all half-Finn." David often speaks as the voice of St. Urho. The following is an excerpt from his website.

Fogey's so proud of his "Bug" he hopes to give it to St. Urho someday! The thing has a wheelbase of a Honda Civic and was built completely from spare parts! It is urged down the road by:

A VW "Bug" front end, Allis Chalmers fenders, "B" John Deere gas tank, wheelchair ramp rollbar, bed-frame motor mounts, manure spreader wheels, an old Ford Bronco frame, '57 Chevy truck trans-

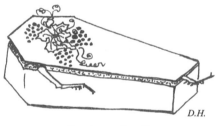

D.H.

Grasshopper's coffin

mission, Canadian Curtis-Wright snowmobile engine, and a Maverick rear-end. ("Can you say dat here? Okay, 'Ford' rear-end!")

It's Practically NEW!

The "Bug" goes 45 miles per hour in wide-open summer, but after about five miles, the pesky plugs melt! It prefers running to the fish-house and towing terrified kids on snow saucers! The thing has sputtered and wheezed its way through countless parades!

Letter to the Editor

Every time a civic problem comes up in Menahga, Minnesota, St. Urho seems to pop up out of nowhere and "yumps all ower" it. Thanks to David Nohrenberg for sharing this letter to the local editor.

Yust Pee4 '95

To ta Ettitor,

Please holt my suppscripsun til Martse peegus my new yearse resolussion! Vee kott pick ruppels — As Menakka's baitrun saint, I feel it's my tudy to boint out an alarming drent in vaistlines tiss vineter! In laymens' derms, effrypuddy iss kedding picker! Minesell inglootett!

How I no tatt? I vots carse! In my pissness eafen suttle tifference in enchine noise leffels. Pumper heights and ant speet fersus tessipellse iss imbortant. Vell, ta carse bumming arount my gorner are slything along like fallen flatprett ant sount like a paritone vootpecker vid asthma! And let's face it, in tiss lufflee vedder, vun can icknore ice pilltup ant vorn out socks.

Not to vurry, Menakka. I kott sloosun! Koase like tiss: "Learn from da plack pair!" In fall, plack pair stuffs himsell to pilt up enerchy for long vinter. At ta first feffy frost, he yust plops hiss oafer-pertenned patootie in a ten, guddles up to ta missus ant toases off.

No tout treaming about nippling pluperrys. Come spring, he's strong assa nox! An tattsitt!

So next dime you kett da uriche to haff a peer or a kopple a beenut pudder samwitts, dake a nap instett. Menakka hassent pen spenting enuff dimes in pett. If neat pee, girl-up in your fisshouse! On your neece, you soot all make New Yearse resoloosun! Hoo else coot tell you tiss?

Ant ven you gum around mine gorner into down, pack off, poika! Urho's hypernating! No need to tank me, Urho.

Likeness of St. Urho Found in Minnesota Rock

From The Review Messenger, *published by Tim Bloomquist, Sebeka, Minnesota. Reprinted with permission.*

A pair of dedicated Finnish "historians," Hugh Mellin and Einar Saarela of New York Mills, Minnesota, were in Sebeka the other day displaying a rock slab which they claim bears a likeness of St. Urho on its surface. The rock was cut open by Sebeka farmer Wesley Ervasti, who in addition to polishing rocks has previously established some notoriety as a "bull shipper," and has a mounted Hereford bull head on display in the Menahga bank.

Ervasti reportedly (the reports are quite vague) found the rock in the vicinity of the Finn Creek Open Air Museum near New York Mills with the aid of a compass which was attracted by the rock's peculiar magnetism, which Ervasti attributes to the legendary saint. When he sawed the rock open, the spirit of the good saint departed, taking with it any traces of magnetism from the rock. However, a faint likeness of Urho's face remains on the rock's surface, he says.

Saarela, who is president of the board of the New York Mills Chapter of the Minnesota Finnish-American Historical Society, which operates the Finn Creek Museum, told us that as "saints are normally buried 30 feet deep, and as all traces of the gravesite have been eroded over the centuries, no plans are being made to attempt to excavate the burial site."

When Jussi Urhonen, chairman of the Menahga St. Urho Statue committee, was informed of the possible finding of St. Urho's final resting place, he said, "There is certainly no point in excavating for possible remains of St. Urho because, as everyone knows, the good saint has risen and is now residing in Menahga!"

Saint Alive and Well

The people of Calumet, Michigan scoff at the rumor of Minnesota's Urho Stone. According to parade director Tom Tikkanen, as quoted in the *Detroit Free Press,* he and some friends found the frozen body of St. Urho and the little sauna stove that had accompanied him across the Atlantic, up the St. Lawrence Seaway, and through the Soo Locks. When they fired up that sauna, St. Urho thawed out just in time for the annual parade!

A Small Miracle

Another of the many wonders performed by St. Urho as originally noted in The Review Messenger, *published by Tim Bloomquist. Reprinted with permission.*

The unknown powers of St. Urho still live on. It seems our local Pastor Luoma sent a St. Urho's Day certificate and card to his parents in Fitchburg, Massachusetts. They thoroughly enjoyed receiving them. However, something strange happened the day after they received the certificate. Mrs. Luoma (Salume) put one of Mr. Luoma's (Toivo's) shirts in the wash. Now that in itself is not unique as Salume often puts Toivo's shirts in the wash, but this time, something unusual happened. To begin with, the shirt was green, but when it came out . . . well, we quote from Salume's letter, and we'll let you be the judge.

Says Salume: "Got the Urho certificate, the Urho *Päivä* card, we really got a lot of chuckles out of them, that is, the things related to St. Urho. This you won't believe, but it is true. Monday morning I did the wash, and I put in a green shirt of Toivo's, and when it came out, it was pink, a sort of lavenderish pink. Dad kiddingly said that was the result of having the St. Urho certificate."

To those who yet doubt, consider the above very carefully!

St. Urho Statue, Take 2

You can never have too much of a good thing. If one Urho statue is good, two are better, or so the folks of Finland, Minnesota must have thought. Carved in 1982 by Don Osborn, the statue was originally planned to be 30 feet tall, but the wood was partially rotted and the carving now stands at 18 feet. Saint Urho has a grasshopper design on his hat and no body.

This wooden carving of St. Urho stands along the Highway 1 entrance to Finland, Minnesota. It is directly across from a chain-saw carving of a fish holding a beer keg. Drive slowly. If you speed through this little village inland from Lake Superior, you may not realize you have been there.

Our Urho

A dedication to the statue by Brenda Van Bergen

Our Urho, Saint that he is,
Bravely stands his ground.
As Finland's protector he's surely a whiz,
And the tallest fellow around.

Sculpted by desire, as is the whole day,
Local artists take their shot.
To show togetherness done Finland's way,
The best natural resource Finland's got!

His woolen hat and stature tall,
Strongly feature his toothy yell.
Grasshopper, grasshopper soon you will fall!
Is the story the statue will tell.

The tribute in our town holds flowers,
The flag, and a Finn.
A more popular guy just won't be found —
He's a symbol of our battle and a win.

Our Urho's deep-lined face
Sees the sun set each day,
Leaving Finland a peaceful place
By protecting us in his own special way.

Queen Helmi Drag Contest

Each year, as part of the St. Urho's Day festivities, the residents of Finland, Minnesota hold the "Queen Helmi Drag Contest" to find the beloved saint a wife. The more outlandish the costume the better, as these pictures show.

Button reflects the theme: St. Urho goes to the movies.

*Above:
Ron Van Bergen, the first Miss Helmi, 1984.*

The 1996 Court Gregory Kellerman, Queen, right, with his attendants: Aaron T. Wilson, James P. Stevens, and David Jokela, all dressed as movie queens.

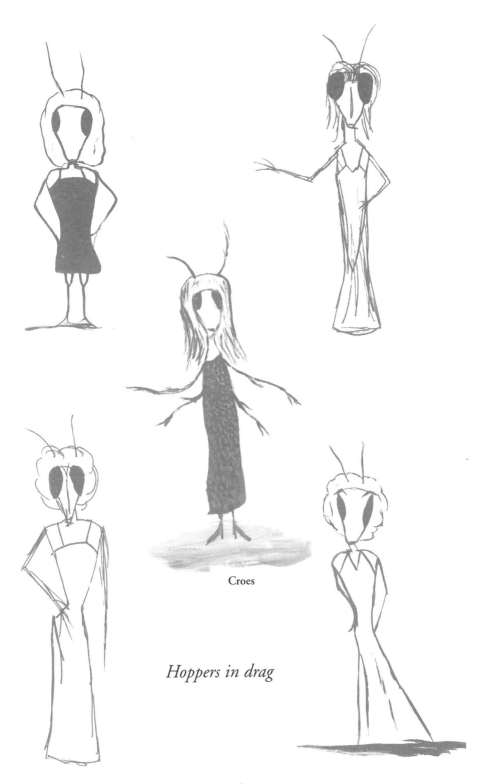

Croes

Hoppers in drag

Street scene in Finland, Minnesota

Grasshopper head made of snow waiting for the spring meltdown.

Wild West theme float created by Brenda Van Bergen for the 1994 St. Urho's Day Parade, Finland, Minnesota. The Iron Range is in northern Minnesota.

A float in the Finland, Minnesota St. Urho's Day Parade

Croes

Hopper taking a sauna.

A Word of Finnish Can Save the Day

by Elizabeth Liiste Kantor

This essay was first published by Finnish-American Heritage in Minneapolis.

My grandpa always said the Dr. Henry Higgins Award should go to St. Urho of Finland. Sure, Eliza Doolittle learned the King's English, but that's not half as difficult as learning Finnish. Look at how many Finns speak English — now look at how many of the British have learned to speak Finnish!

Of course, St. Urho is special in that he saved Finland from a plague of grasshoppers through his language skills. It was the summer of 1827, just when everyone in Turku was getting set to pick the new grape crop, when the grasshoppers arrived in droves and began devouring the fruit. The polite Finns tried talking to the hoppers and asked them to refrain from eating the grapes. All they did was chomp and talk with their mouths full.

Urho was a young boy who knew how rude it was to talk with one's mouth full, so he chided the grasshoppers for their lack of manners. Getting into a conversation with the hoppers, he asked where they were from and didn't they know that *"Oma koti kullan kallis?"* (That translates to "home sweet home.") The grasshoppers said they didn't have a home. Oh, they remembered during Pharaoh Ramses II's reign that they lived in Egypt, but they had been on the move ever since. Now here in Finland the grapes tasted so good that maybe they would make this their home.

That gave Urho a plan to save Finland. "If you want to live here, you'll have to learn how to speak Finnish properly — none of this Fingliska!" he said. "Tonight, I'll teach you. Meet me at the revolving outdoor theatre after dinner."

Well, the hoppers arrived with very full stomachs, and they rudely jammed themselves into the theatre seats, pushing out the people. Urho got on stage and had the hoppers practice saying things like *Tervetuloa! Mitä kuuluu? Anteeksi!* and *Kiitos!* They complained how difficult it was to say such polite things, but Urho made them practice so hard that they sprained their tongues. While they were trying to regain the use of their voices, Urho shouted, *"Mene hiiteen heinäsirkka!"* and had the theatre revolve faster and faster until a vortex built up to such a force that the hoppers were whirled into the eye of a tornado and spun out of the country. The frantic revolving caused sparks to fly, and a fire broke out and burned down almost the whole of Turku (fortunately, the cathedral didn't burn nor the grape crop). In its wake the inhabitants found a batch of roasted grasshoppers which they said went well with their newly brewed wine. To this day, where grasshoppers are found, you'll notice that they can communicate only by rubbing their hind legs together.

The moral of St. Urho's Day being: One must learn the customs of one's new country if one is to be welcomed and be made at home. By the way, Grandpa had the year of St. Urho's feat right, almost all of Turku did burn in 1827. Check any history book.

D.H.

Hapless grasshoppers being spun out of Finland in a vortex.

My Career as St. Urho's Disciple

by Janice Laulainen

Someone told me once that the Finns are a dying breed. Well, St. Urho and St. Urho's Day are a Finn-Fun way to keep our heritage alive and long remembered! I've been a disciple of St. Urho for thirty years, since 1970. I joined The Finnish-American Heritage in Minneapolis with a lifetime membership. I was Secretary of The Finnish-American Heritage in Minneapolis for twenty years. There I learned about St. Urho, and I started cutting out *heinäsirkkas* (grasshoppers) for name tags for their St. Urho's Day celebration. I was converted and hooked that very first year! I've been cutting out grasshoppers every year since.

I feel the same way as the priest quoted by Clarence Ivonen:
"In these troubled times, we need all the Saints we can muster."

I believe in enjoying life, my heritage and promoting a good time for others. My grandparents came from Finland and were married here. My father was the only boy, youngest of five children. He couldn't speak any English until he was six and started school. Sometimes I think my mother felt slighted because I am so into my Finnish heritage. My mother is German. I've been to Finland four times: 1971, 1974, 1976 and 1992 to visit second cousins. It's interesting when I talk to non-Finns; most of them say they know at least one Finn, since Minnesota has over 100,000 Finnish Americans.

Prior to my father's stroke in 1994, I was very active for twenty-four years with the Finnish-American St. Urho celebrations. We had contests every year to crown a St. Urho. The contestants had 30 seconds to make a grape necklace with real grapes using a needle and thread; dip a sock into grape juice and the one who squeezed the most grape juice from the sock was our St. Urho; with their bare foot, pick out rubber grasshoppers from a bunch of grapes, hop like a grasshopper and chant: *"Heinäsirkka, Heinäsirkka, mene täältä hiiteen!"* or compete in a grape eating contest, etc. Several television

Janice in her decorated office at Dayton's.

stations interviewed me when I was in my costume. I wrote to the Action News station telling them that I had the "Grasshopper Blues," as I could not find any chocolate-covered grasshoppers for our celebration. They followed up on it for two nights. The University of Minnesota said that they would make them for us, but they were out of season in March. Lunds Grocery said they could order them from France at a cost of $1,000. I even wrote to President Urho Kekkonen in Finland and the Johnny Carson show. The outcome: a Minneapolis department store gourmet shop donated a can of fried grasshoppers! Since we visit my father daily at the Care Center, I now devote my time and energy to decorating my office at Dayton's Department Store, and sending fun brochures that I put together each year to help the media give mention of SUD (St. Urho's Day).

It takes me two to three hours to decorate my office in purple, green, grasshoppers, and grapes. Employees look forward to it each year. I have contests (Guess how many grape Tootsie Rolls are in the jar; name the grasshopper, etc.) and give prizes such as a large bottle of grape juice or grape jelly. My neighbor, a Danish lady who is ninety-six years old, for years has knitted purple and green slippers, mug rugs, little baskets, etc., to use for my display and/or prizes. I serve Keebler Grasshopper cookies. I dress in my purple wig, suit, buttons, grape slippers (which I found at Dayton's as well as grasshopper napkins). A lady on the escalator asked: "What do they pay you to wear that?" When the day is done, I take some of my decorations to the Care Center and celebrate with my eighty-six year old father and the other residents. They love it! I make all non-Finns honorary Finns on St. Urho's Day. The enthusiasm is contagious, and I hope the younger generation will continue to keep St. Urho's Day and our Finnish heritage alive.

Elmer Kemppainen, principal of Cooper High School, for many years before he retired, held a St. Urho Breakfast for friends and school staff at 5:30 a.m. on the morning of the 16th. They served green scrambled eggs, rolls with purple frosting, and grape juice. The teachers put on skits about St. Urho. They were referred to as

Photo by Janice Laulainen

Standing in for the real saint is David Kallio at a Minneapolis St. Urho's Day celebration.

the Hysterical St. Urho Fans and Finns. It was a great way to start the day. I always provided brochures about the saint and his holiday.

WCCO 830 Radio in Minneapolis has been instrumental in getting St. Urho's Day off the ground since the early 1970s. I have dropped off Keebler Grasshopper cookies, grape juice, and grape candies with my brochures each year, and they have responded to this Finn-Fun by playing the *Ballad of St. Urho* and the *St. Urho Polka* on the radio. The night receptionist even called one day and asked me to pick up my grasshopper. She had made me a large green grasshopper ceramic planter with purple and green flowers! I still use it as a table decoration. When I was interviewed at the Minnesota State Fair by Roger Erickson, WCCO 830 Radio, he asked about the slogan for St. Urho. I chanted: *"Heinäsirkka, Heinäsirkka, mene täältä hiiteen!"* ("Grasshopper, Grasshopper, go away!") He thought at first that I swore at him! With Urho meaning hero, I told Roger that I call Minnesota *Urho Country*! My Irish friend at Dayton's dresses in purple and green to celebrate March 16 St. Urho's Day; then she celebrates March 17 St. Patrick's Day. I tell people that on March 17, I become O'Laulainen.

A poster describing the "kill" of a 23-lb. grasshopper hangs in Janice Laulainen's office for St. Urho's Day at Dayton's.

We've Come a Long Way, Urho Baby!

Rob Hotakainen, formerly of Lakes Publishing in Detroit Lakes, Minnesota, and more recently with the Fergus Falls Daily Journal, wrote these reflections of what it means to be Finnish in America. Reprinted with permission.

Some basic and fundamental human tenets:

We live in an assimilated society, often overlooking the traits and idiosyncrasies of the various ethnic groups that have shaped the United States of America into the great country that it is today.

But, thankfully, times are changing. Credit is finally being given where credit is due. We have come to recognize and appreciate:

- That it was the Germans who gave us polkas and beer;
- That it was the Poles who gave us jokes and laughter;
- That it was the Irish who gave us potatoes and Irish whiskey;
- That it was the Swedes who gave us blondes and Volvos;
- That it was the English who gave us Worcestershire sauce;
- That it was the Norwegians who gave us sardines;
- That it was the Dutch who gave us tulips;
- That it was the French who gave us frog legs;
- That it was the Russians who gave us male ballerinas;
- That it was the Danes who gave us pastry;
- That it was the Italians who gave us garlic;
- And, finally, it was the Hungarians who gave us the Gabor sisters.

That's fine and dandy. These ethnic groups have left their mark, and historians will duly record their contributions. They are significant in that they have contributed to the wholesomeness of the country at large.

But let's get down to the nuts and bolts of the matter at hand: Where would the country be without the Finns?

It is a deeply sobering question. It is a question that tires the mind, a question that no mortal man can fully answer.

There are some who acclaim the Finns as the most intelligent and diverse people to ever inhabit Planet Earth. But, admittedly, there are others who have not yet come to grips with this basic and fundamental human tenet. Most reasonable Americans have come to understand, however, that Finns have earned, and deserve, the distinction of being on top in modern society's echelons.

Outlining the virtues of the Finns could fill up this entire magazine; so for brevity's sake we will mention only the obvious.

Consider, if you will, the impact the Finns have had on this country:

- It was the Finns who discovered that it's possible to eat fish and spit the bones out of the sides of their mouths. While this may

D.H.

Celebrating St. Urho's Day in grasshopper costume

seem insignificant on the surface, it actually helped bring about the true democratic spirit of tolerance. Anyone who can watch such a sight can surely be tolerant of a few pinkos.

- It was the Finns who discovered flatbread. Finally, bread did not have to be packaged in a large and clumsy package. The Finns understood that small is beautiful. Breakthroughs in the packaging industry ensued and eventually climaxed by the selling of pantyhose in plastic eggshells.

- It was the Finns who discovered the sauna. (And please, that's pronounced *sowna,* not *saw-na.*) Finns are well-known for taking a sauna and then jumping into a lake or rolling in the snow to cool off. Simply, it was the Finns who understood that cold should follow hot. Or even more simply, that opposites attract. This breakthrough may also seem insignificant, but the same reasoning eventually led to the hot fudge sundae.

- It was the Finns who gave their children names like Eino, Reino, and Toivo. Again, this may seem insignificant, but it was the Finns who sustained the American spirit of individuality. By refusing to name their children Tom, Dick and Harry, they demonstrated that standing alone means standing free, and forever repeating how your name is spelled.

One could go on and on, but the point is clear; the world is, without a doubt, a better place because of the Finns.

That's why we pay tribute to the most famous Finn of them all: St. Urho. He is the patron saint of the Finns, and he stands tall and free in downtown Menahga. He bettered mankind by saving Finland's grapes and wine industry from an infestation of grasshoppers. He is recognized as the epitome of the Finnish character. He was a true patriot.

At long last, there stands a Finn that is larger than life itself. It's about time. This country has come a long way, Baby.

The Order of St. Urho

In recent years a number of St. Urho fan clubs and associations have sprung up across the country, including the "Nytes" of St. Urho and Urho's Boys. Some of these are little more than an excuse to get together with friends, drink purple beer, and swap tall tales. Others are more elaborate, as this pledge from the Order of St. Urho shows.

The illustrious, indefatigable, noble, courageous, exuberant, lively, hilarious, gallant, renown, celebrated, intrepid, merry, fearless

Order of St. Urho

Tiss is tu sertivy tat

---

haffing vorssvoolee panished krassoppers vit tose immortall vords, *"Heinäsirkka, heinäsirkka, mene täältä hiiteen"* an haffing kvafft ta joose of ta krape, is herepy inwested vit ta order of St. Urho.

Hii or Sii iss herepy:

I. Empowwart vit Suomalainen sisu.
II. Kranted ta rite tu:
    a. Tell Finn yokes vitout askin.
    b. Peek Finglish.
    c. Panish krassoppers on rekvest.
    d. Yuus anni sauna vitout askin.
    e. Pay taiss to Suomi instead upp ta U.S., if hii vant tu.
    f. Sarge at ta Co-op tori vitout limit.

Maaliskuu 16, 2000
St. Urho and the Finnish American Heritage
Perinnöllinen Suomalainen

Thanks to Janice Laulainen for providing the text.

"Grape" Things to Do on Saint Urho's Day

- Chant *"Heinäsirkka, Heinäsirkka, mene täältä hiiteen!"* ("Grasshopper, Grasshopper, Go Away!")
- Toast St. Urho with a glass of grape juice.
- Have a grape toss.
- Make a real grape necklace.
- Squeeze grape juice from a sock.
- Go out and catch some grasshoppers.
- Have someone feed you grapes.
- Guess how many grapes are in a bunch.
- Eat some Grape Nuts.
- Name a grasshopper.
- Have a piece of Grasshopper Pie.
- Have a Keebler Grasshopper Cookie.
- Eat a chocolate-covered grasshopper.
- Have a Grasshopper made from ice cream.
- Spit grape seeds in the sauna.
- Hop like a grasshopper.
- Make grape Jello.
- Make a grasshopper out of green plastic bags.
- Try a grape or grasshopper lollipop.
- Make a grasshopper bar.
- Wear purple and green.
- Draw a grape and a grasshopper.
- Dye your hair purple and green.
- Dance the St. Urho Polka.
- Do the Grape Shuffle.
- Tell everyone to have a "Grape Day."
- Visit St. Urho statues in Menahga and Finland, Minnesota.
- Play Parker Brothers' Grape Escape Game.
- Join the Royal Order of St. Urho.
- Make a St. Urho's Day greeting card.
- Read "A Tale for St. Urho's Tay."

Have a Finn-Fun Finntastic day!
Yours in Grasshoppers and Grapes, Janice Laulainen

St. Urho's Day
Memorial Chemistry Experiment
by Harold Westron, Chemistry Teacher
Bloomington High School, Bloomington, Minnesota

The purpose of this experiment is to celebrate the memory of St. Urho and his great deeds. The magnitude of the conflict between good and evil will be illustrated dramatically. From the archives of Janice Laulainen.

To do this experiment with the proper attitude of reverence, first recite the "Ode to St. Urho" (from memory) and then enter the laboratory in a meditative mood. Silence is needed for the proper atmosphere of contemplation.

Begin by filling test tubes with Finnish Grape Juice as indicated: (Test Tube 1: full; Test Tube 2: 1/2 full; Test Tube 3: 1/10 full). Fill a beaker about 1/2 full of this same solution and invert Test Tube 1 (cover open end with thumb) in the beaker. With forceps, reverently remove a grasshopper egg from bottle at center of the table and gently place in the beaker. Move Test Tube 1 over the egg to collect any gaseous product. When test tube is filled with this product, remove it and, keeping it mouth down, insert a burning splint. Repeat procedure with Test Tubes 2 and 3. Record all observations.

In your lab report form, respond to the following questions:

1. Why did the results of the "burning splint test" differ in Test Tubes 1, 2, and 3?

2. Discuss the results of this experiment as it relates to St. Urho's struggle against the grasshoppers. Include the significance of color changes, energy released, etc.

After completion of the laboratory work, return to the classroom to celebrate St. Urho's Day with your favorite classmates, friends, chemistry teacher, and St. Urho!

St. Urho's Day Games

Photo by John Johnson

One of the St. Urho's Day traditions in Menahga, Minnesota is the "Changing of the Guard" where participants strip down and exchange their elaborately decorated long johns.

D.H.

Red Flannel Run

The town of Roy, Minnesota celebrates St. Urho's Day with "The Red Flannel Run," when participants, dressed in red long johns, sprint down the middle of the street toward the "Finnish" line.

Grape-on-a-Spoon Race

In Northville, New York, they combine the Nordic sport of skiing with the celebration of St. Urho. The premiere event is the "Grape-on-a-Spoon Race," where you must ski the entire cross-country ski course without dropping your grape. There is even a three-legged ski race where you are tied to your partner's leg while skiing! More traditional Finnish games do take place, including the "Arctic Sled Ride," where you zoom around the lake tied to a pole in the center, as well as *kyykkä*, a type of ice bowling.

Lawn-Mower Races

Another popular Saint Urho's Day contest held in parts of Minnesota and Michigan is the "Riding Lawn-Mower Race" — but if there's a mid-March snow, this isn't always possible!

Queen for a Day

Many communities celebrate by picking a St. Urho's Day Queen (or if you're in Finland, Minnesota, that's a Drag Queen). In Hood River, Oregon, they crown their queen with a wreath of plastic grasshoppers as members of the Finnish Women's Drill Team swirl Finnish flags attached to power drills.

Donut Seeds

The folks at Suomi College in Michigan serve "donut seeds" at their St. Urho celebration. These seeds — which look remarkably like Cheerios — can be taken home and planted in the garden. With luck, by next St. Urho's Day there will be donuts ripe for the picking.

Wife Carrying

The celebrations in Roy, Minnesota also include a "Wife Carrying Race." A contestant has to carry his wife through an obstacle course — through a lineup of old tires, up and over snowbanks, around barrels and back again to the starting line — hopefully without dropping his wife in the process! If a gentlemen doesn't have a wife, no problem, he can purchase a 30-minute marriage license for $1.00, just enough time to take part in the race.

There is a similar event held at the Lapland Lake Cross Country Ski Center in Northville, New York, where they claim the origins of the event come from the Finnish tradition of stealing your wife-to-be under cover of night. It is a 40-yard race with only one rule, "You must run the entire course with your wife in the air — how you do it is up to you." There are no handicaps awarded for lighter or heavier wives.

Fitzsimmons
From Joyful Nordic Humor

A New Twist to Some Old Favorites

Grapescotch

You probably played hopscotch as a kid, but by now you've probably forgotten most of the basic rules — and I'll bet you have never played it quite like this!

You will need: Chalk or masking tape; LARGE grapes; small stuffed grasshopper for a prize.

Draw a hopscotch pattern using grape and grasshopper designs on the sidewalk. If you're indoors, use masking tape to mark out the design. The first player tosses a grape onto the first circle, then hops over the first spot to the second circle. You must land on one foot! Continue hopping from one circle to the next until you can land on the grasshopper with both feet. Shout, *"Heinäsirkka, heinäsirkka, mene täältä hiiteen!"* Reverse the hops, bending down to scoop up the grape. From there hop out. If you make it all the way through, toss the grape onto the second circle and repeat. If the grape doesn't land in the proper spot or if you fall and lose your balance, it's the next person's turn. A prize goes to the first person who can make it through.

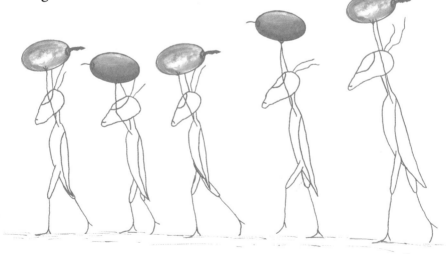

Croes

Grape, Grape, Grasshopper!

If you grew up in the Upper Midwest, you might remember this game as "Duck Duck Goose" or "Duck Duck Grey Duck." Everyone except the person who is "it" sits in a circle facing each other. The person who is "it" walks around the outside of the circle. If you are "it," tap each person on the head and say "grape." Keep saying "grape" until you choose a person to be "grasshopper." When someone is tapped as the grasshopper, he gets up and chases you around the circle. He will try to tag you before you can get back to his spot. If he does tag you, you will have to start over again. If you make it to the grasshopper's spot, he is now "it."

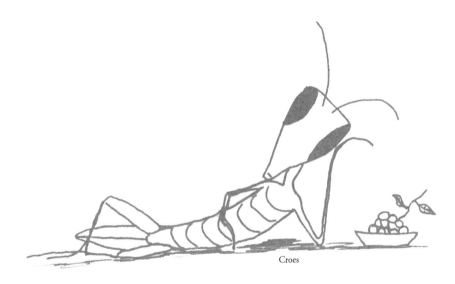

Croes

Indolent grasshopper eating grapes.

Pin the Grasshopper on Saint Urho's Nose
You will need:
- A picture of St. Urho
- A cut-out of a bunch of grapes or a grasshopper
- A blindfold
- Thumbtacks

Tape the picture of St. Urho to the wall. Each player has a turn and is blindfolded and spun in a circle three times clockwise and three times counterclockwise. He/she is then pointed in the general direction of St. Urho. The goal is to pin the grasshopper over the tip of the saint's nose. Whoever is closest wins.

St. Urho's Day Green and Purple Party Ideas
By Diane Heusinkveld

All legends need children to continue traditions for the next generation. They love parties, and making the goodies. Here are a few ideas to start, then let your creative side experiment. Twist green streamers together like grape vines with bunches of purple balloons as grapes. Let the children help decide how many and where.

Celery Hoppers: Mix cream cheese with green food coloring. Fill 3-inch pieces of celery with the cheese. Place two raisins for eyes and two half pieces of pretzel sticks as legs.

Hopper Legs: Melt white chocolate in double boiler, adding green food coloring until reaching desired shade. Dip a pretzel once, coating all except 1/8 inch at one end to hold on to. Cool a few seconds between each dip, then re-dip several more times, dipping slightly shallower each time to build up the leg to look like shape shown. Cool on rack and serve pretzel end up in small glasses.

Green and Purple Jello: Mix lime and grape Jello in separate bowls as stated on box for molded Jello. Chill until slightly thickened. Stir green grapes into purple grape Jello and purple grapes into lime Jello. Spoon into clear disposable cups, layering half of each color. Chill 2 hours.

Purple and Green Punch:
2 qts. bottled grape juice (purple or green) 1 sliced lime
2 qts. sparkling water or club soda   grapes (green & purple)
1 qt. lemon-lime soda   2 qts. ice cubes
At serving time mix all except lime slices and grapes. Float fruit on top. Freeze grapes into ice cubes if desired. Ice cubes can be made of lime and grape Kool-aid or fruit juice, as cubes or in gelatin molds.

Fun Grasshopper Facts

Amaze and dazzle your friends with these little-known facts about grasshoppers. Create your own version of Trivial Pursuit at your next St. Urho gathering.

Grasshopper: "Grasshopper" is the common name for plant-eating orthopterous insects with hind legs adapted for jumping, including long-horned grasshoppers and locusts. They sometimes engage in migratory flights of destruction, eating their way through entire crops.

Distribution: Worldwide

Habitat: As the name suggests, most grasshoppers can be found in grassy meadows, fields and hedges.

Color: Green or brown or greenish-brown. Some species go through a seasonal color change, from green to reddish brown.

Length: Grasshoppers can grow up to 3 inches, but most are between 1/2 inch and 1-1/8 inches.

Metamorphosis: Although some of the more than 5,000 species of grasshoppers are wingless, most have well-developed wings. Initially wingless, grasshopper nymphs go through several molts until they are fully grown. Only the adults can fly.

- Grasshoppers are active during the day; if disturbed they will leap away with the help of their oversized hind legs.

- A grasshopper can jump 20 times the length of its own body. It's not surprising that the grasshopper can jump so far; it has 100 more muscles than a human being.

- Grasshoppers can travel long distances with the help of the wind. They will travel for miles in the same direction as they search for food.

- Grasshoppers are herbivorous, feeding on grass and leaves, but when food is scarce they will eat almost anything. There are stories of grasshoppers eating straw hats left in fields — and even old pitchfork handles!

- Grasshoppers have one large compound eye on each side of their heads, so they can see in the front, back and sides. They also have three single eyes, but scientists aren't sure about the purpose of these eyes.

- The chirping sound they make is called grasshopper stridulation. A row of tiny, evenly spaced pegs on their hind legs is rubbed over the veins or ribs of the forewing. Usually only the males can sing, and each species has its own song.

- Grasshoppers have a number of enemies, including mice, birds, spiders and snakes. Some insects, such as flies, will even lay their eggs on a grasshopper's body.

- When a grasshopper is picked up, its defense is to spit a brown liquid. That's probably why they're always depicted in cartoons as chewing tobacco.

- The Bible mentions grasshoppers and locusts a total of thirty-eight times and has nine different names for referring to these creatures: arbeh, chagab, chargol, chasil, gazam, gob, sal'am, tze-latzal and yelek.

A Miracle in Minnesota

Grasshopper, Grasshopper . . . tales abound about the plague of these voracious plant-eaters. Janice Laulainen, St. Urho historian, calls attention to the "Grasshopper Chapel" near Cold Spring, Minnesota. There one can see the structure dedicated to the Virgin Mary.

The story began in 1877 when the crops of the German-Catholic immigrants were plagued by locusts. They beseeched Mary for help in getting rid of the hoppers, promising to build a church in her honor if their wish was granted. As legend has it, the swarm of grasshoppers was gone the next day!

As promised, the farmers kept their pledge and the church was built, but in 1894 a tornado struck the area. The church was picked up and flung into the nearby trees. (Some say this explains why the trees around the chapel continue to grow at odd angles.)

The legend survived, but it was not until 1951 that the chapel was reconstructed and was consecrated a year later. Inside is a statue of Mary that is from the original structure. Outside, above the door, is a figure of Mary gazing down at two grasshoppers who seem to be giving her a boost toward heaven.

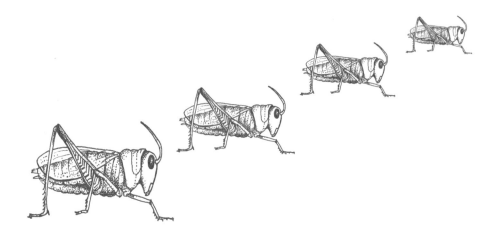

St. Urho's Grasshopper Quilt Blocks

by Joanne Asala

Donna Dawson Asala became an honorary Finn when she married my father, Ronald. She began quilting in 1996 with The Grandma Quilt, sewn from blocks her mother had started more than fifty years ago. It's her goal to make a quilt for every child in the family — and with all the nieces, nephews, grandchildren, and cousins we have — it will take her quite a while!

While Donna has made a number of quilts from traditional patterns, including the popular Double Wedding Ring, she has also created several quilts of original design. These often feature animals or popular folklore motifs. Her Urho's Grasshopper quilt blocks, featured on the back cover, are the first quilt blocks to explore Finnish themes. (Instructions are on following pages.)

Urho's Grasshopper Quilt Block
by Donna Asala

"Finnished" block size 9 x 9 inches

For one quilt block you will need:
    1 "fat" quarter-yard fabric with grape pattern
    1 "fat" quarter-yard fabric of purple pattern
    Scraps of green fabric for hopper
    "Heat 'n' Bond" or other fusible fabric backing
    Gold, white, and black fabric paint
    Fine paintbrush
    Optional: If you want to machine-applique the hoppers, a matching or contrasting thread is needed. A zigzag or button-hole stitch works well.

You will need to cut two square pieces from the grape-pattern fabric: one 7-1/2 x 7-1/2 inches, the other 4-1/2 x 4-1/2 inches. (Allowances have already been added for a 1/4-inch seam.)

From the purple fabric cut a 9 x 9-inch square.

Take the smaller of the grape fabric squares and draw a diagonal line from one corner to the opposite. This will be your stitch line. Pin this block to the 9 x 9-inch block. Machine-stitch or hand-sew along your sewing line. Trim to a 1/4-inch seam and press open. Repeat with the 7-1/2 x 7-1/2-inch square, attaching it to the main piece of fabric.

Press the "Heat 'n' Bond" or other fusible fabric to the wrong side of the green fabric you intend to use. Trace the hopper body pieces to the right side of the fabric using a "disappearing ink" pen. Cut out the pieces. Remove the paper backing on the "Heat 'n' Bond" and arrange the hopper pieces in the center of your quilt block. Press them down. Use the fabric paints to outline the hopper, adding eyes, antenna, etc. When paint is dry you are ready to frame your block!

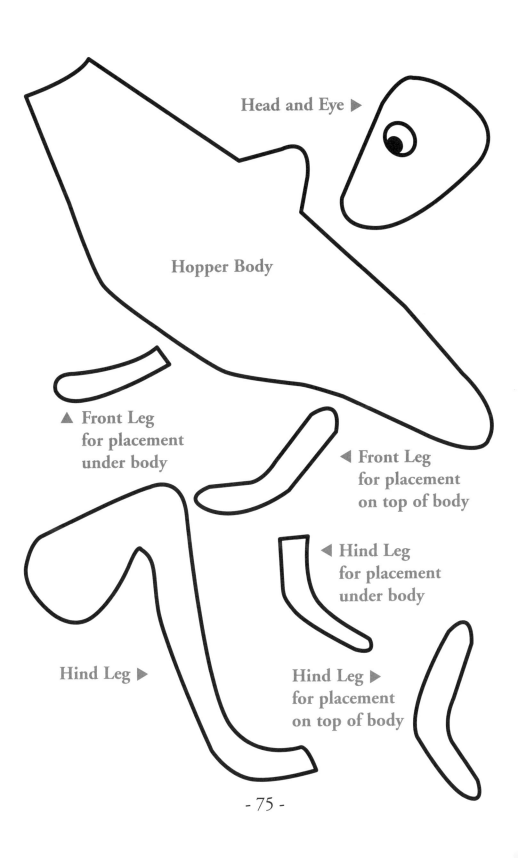

Head and Eye ▶

Hopper Body

▲ Front Leg
for placement
under body

◀ Front Leg
for placement
on top of body

◀ Hind Leg
for placement
under body

Hind Leg ▶

Hind Leg ▶
for placement
on top of body

Food Fit for a Saint

"Of these you may eat any kind of locust, katydid, cricket or grasshopper."
—Leviticus 11:22

According to the "Ode to St. Urho" by Mrs. Gene McCavic, eating hearty dishes of viiliä *made this "praff Finn" both "tall unt trong." He also ate* kalamojakka, *a type of fish stew, every hour so he'd have the strength to do his chores. The following two recipes come from the cookbook of my great-grandmother, Agnes Marta Aelstadt Soby. In 1913, at the age of seventeen, she emigrated alone from Helsinki to Chicago.*

Marta's "Viili"

2 tablespoons viili starter (or
    2 tablespoons buttermilk)
1/4 cup milk,
    room temperature

1/4 cup cream,
    room temperature
Salt to taste
Brown sugar, cinnamon, berries
    (optional)

Combine viili starter, milk, and cream in a small bowl. Cover loosely with a dishcloth and leave overnight in a warm, preferably dark place. Don't move it, and don't peek! It should thicken to the consistency of Jello (if you haven't shaken it, that is). If not, leave it to set a while longer until it coagulates. Take a few tablespoons and set aside as starter. Chill the rest for an hour. Season with salt to taste. For a sweeter version, sprinkle with brown sugar, cinnamon, and fresh berries. Serves 1.

Finnish Coffee Bread "Pulla"

St. Urho's Day is a good time to introduce your friends to pulla, *a traditional sweet bread served with coffee.*

1 package active dry yeast
1/2 cup warm water
2 cups milk, scalded and cooled to lukewarm
1-1/2 cups sugar, less if preferred
1 teaspoon salt

8 whole cardamom pods, seeded and crushed (1 tablespoon)
4 eggs, beaten
8 to 9 cups flour, divided
1/2 cup melted butter, divided

Glaze:
1 egg, beaten
1 teaspoon coffee

1/2 cup crushed lump sugar
1/2 cup sliced almonds

Dissolve the yeast in the warm water. Stir the milk, sugar, salt, cardamom, and eggs into the yeast mixture. Add enough flour to make a batter (about 2 cups worth). Beat until the dough is smooth and elastic. Add about 3 cups of the flour and beat well; the dough should be quite smooth and glossy in appearance. Add 1/2 of the melted butter and stir in well. Beat again until the dough looks glossy. Alternately stir in the remaining flour and butter until a stiff dough forms.

Turn out onto a lightly floured board and cover with an inverted mixing bowl. Let the dough rest 15 minutes, then knead until smooth and satiny. Place in a lightly greased mixing bowl, turn the dough to grease the top, cover lightly, and let rise in a warm place until doubled (about 30 minutes). Punch down and let rise again another 30 minutes until nearly doubled.

Turn out again onto a lightly floured board, divide into 3 parts, then divide each of these parts into thirds. Roll dough between the palms of your hands to form strips. Braid three of the strips together into a straight loaf, pinch the ends together, and tuck under. Repeat for the second and third loaves. Lift the braids onto lightly greased baking sheets. Let rise about 20 minutes until puffy. They will not be doubled in size.

Mix coffee with beaten egg, and glaze the loaves by brushing with the egg and coffee mixture, and if you wish, sprinkle with almonds and sugar.

Bake at 400° for 30 minutes. Do not over bake or the loaves will be too dry. Remove from the oven when a light golden brown. Makes 3 braids. Slice to serve.

Green Hopper Buns Using "Pulla" Dough

After bread dough has risen once, punch down. Make oblong pieces of dough three inches long for body parts, one inch for heads and legs according to size desired. Let rise 20 minutes. Mix egg white with four drops of green food coloring and brush onto hoppers. Sprinkle with green decorator sugar and bake at 375° for approximately 20 minutes.

D.H.

Chocolate-covered Grasshoppers

When I was in college at the University of Iowa, I was served a batch of chocolate-chip cookies that I thought, for sure, contained nuts — but I was wrong! The crunchy little bits were, in fact, oven-dried grasshoppers. The following recipe gives instructions for the general method of preparing grasshoppers, crickets, and other insects. Chop them up in bits and add them to your favorite cookie recipe or dip them in chocolate. Like lobster and other shellfish, they are best when fresh.

24 live grasshoppers
2 squares semi-sweet or dark chocolate

Pour the live grasshoppers into a colander and cover with cheese-cloth. Rinse them with lukewarm water and place in the freezer. After 20 minutes or so they will be dead, but not frozen. Take the grasshopper heads between your forefinger and thumb and gently pull. Also remove wings and hind legs. Spread them out on a cookie sheet and bake at 200° for 2 hours, until they are dried. For every two dozen insects you have, you'll need 2 squares of semi-sweet or dark chocolate. Melt the chocolate and carefully dip grasshoppers. Place on waxed paper and refrigerate. Serves 24, but are you really going to find 24 people to try this?

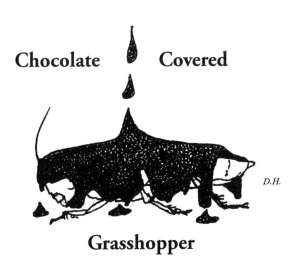

Chocolate   Covered

D.H.

Grasshopper

St. Urho's Fish Stew

6 large potatoes, pared,
   cut into chunks
1 large onion, diced
2 teaspoons salt
5 whole allspice
6 cups water

3 pounds cleaned freshwater fish
   (i.e. trout, walleye, whitefish)
2 cups cream or 1 can (13 oz.)
   undiluted evaporated milk
2 tablespoons butter
Dill to taste

Into large soup kettle, put potatoes, onion, salt, allspice and water. Cover and bring to a boil. Simmer 15 to 20 minutes until potatoes are tender. Cut fish into 2-inch chunks. Lower fish into pot with the potatoes, cover and simmer 15 minutes until fish flakes when probed with a fork. Stew should not boil; fish should remain in rather large pieces (if overcooked it falls apart). Add cream, butter and dill weed if desired. Serve hot. Makes 6 servings.

D.H.

Grasshopper in my soup

Waiter, there's a grasshopper in my soup!

Eating bugs is officially called "entomophagy." Of all insects, grasshoppers are the most commonly consumed bug the world over. Although, nowadays they are sold only in gourmet food shops, hoppers were once eaten by Native-American tribes and early European settlers. They were oftentimes dried and served whole or ground into flour and used in a variety of recipes. They are high in protein, nearly 15 grams for a large hopper, and low in fat. Almost the perfect food! For a St. Urho's Day feast they'll talk about for years, why not try some of the following recipes. If grasshoppers aren't native to your area, contact your local pet supply house or herpetological center. They often sell grasshoppers and crickets as food for pet snakes and turtles.

Grasshopper Stew

My grandfather, Lon Dawson, is editing a recipe collection of meals and rations served to armies and navies throughout history. He's come across a number of dishes that range from the merely strange to the downright bizarre. In the seventeenth-century journal of William Dampier, the first European to discover Australia, he came across the following tasty dish. It seems that when rations were low, sailors ate whatever was at hand! With a little adaptation, it would make a tasty St. Urho's Day supper.

"They had another Dish made of a sort of Locusts, whose Bodies were about an Inch and a half long, and as thick as the top of one's little Finger; with large thin Wings, and long and small Legs. . . .The Natives would go out with small Nets, and take a Quart at one sweep. When they had enough, they would . . . parch them over the Fire in an earthen Pan; their Wings and Legs would fall off, and their Heads and Backs would turn red like boil'd Shrimps. . . .Their Bodies being full, would eat very moist, their Heads would crackle in one's Teeth. I did once eat of this Dish, and liked it well enough."

Chocolate Chip Grasshopper Cookies

2 sticks butter
1 (3-oz.) package cream cheese
1/2 cup sugar
1/2 cup brown sugar
2 eggs
3 tablespoons grated orange rind
1/2 cup crushed dry, roasted
  grasshoppers (see Chocolate
  Covered Grasshopper recipe)

1 tablespoon vanilla
2 cups flour
1 teaspoon baking soda
1 teaspoon salt
1 (12-oz.) package semi-sweet
  chocolate chips

Beat butter, cream cheese, and sugars until fluffy. Add eggs, orange rind, grasshoppers, and vanilla. Beat well. Add flour, baking soda and salt. Stir in chocolate chips. Drop by teaspoonfuls onto a greased cookie sheet and bake for 10–12 minutes at 350°. Yields 5 dozen.

D.H.

Grasshopper Caramel Corn

"And John was clothed with camel's hair, and with a girdle of a skin about his loins; and he did eat grasshoppers and wild honey."

—*Mark 1:6*

10 cups popped corn
1 cup dry-roasted grasshoppers, crushed
1/2 cup butter

1/4 cup corn syrup
1 cup packed brown sugar
1/2 teaspoon salt
1/2 teaspoon baking soda

Pop corn and pour into an oven-proof container; add grasshoppers. Combine butter, corn syrup, sugar and salt in a medium saucepan. Heat over medium flame until bubbly around edges, stirring occasionally. Continue to cook for 5 minutes over medium heat. Remove from flame and add baking soda. Stir until foamy; mixture will double in size. Pour over popped corn. Mix well. Bake at 200° for 1 hour, stirring every 10 minutes. Serves 4.

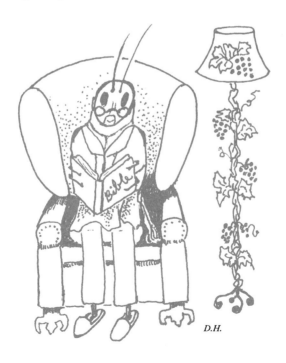

D.H.

Grasshopper Fritters

Wake your family up on St. Urho's m⌐rn with the delicious smell of grasshopper fritters. Modify your fa ⌐rite apple fritter recipe, or use this one. Delicious with a hint of powdered sugar!

2–3 cups fresh grasshoppers, wings and hind legs removed
1 tablespoon rum
3 eggs, separated
1 cup all-purpose flour
1 tablespoon sugar
1/8 teaspoon salt
1/2 cup beer
1-1/2 cups vegetable oil for frying
Powdered sugar, cinnamon-sugar, or maple syrup

Sprinkle grasshoppers with rum and set aside. In a large bowl, mix egg yolks, flour, sugar and salt until just combined. Batter will be lumpy. Add beer and mix until smooth. Set aside to rest for 1 hour. In a separate bowl, beat egg whites until stiff peaks form. Gently fold into beer mixture. Heat oil until very hot. Dip grasshoppers into batter and fry until golden brown, about 4 minutes per side. Flip to make sure they are evenly browned. Remove with a slotted spoon and transfer to a paper towel-lined plate. Sprinkle with powdered sugar, cinnamon-sugar, and/or maple syrup.

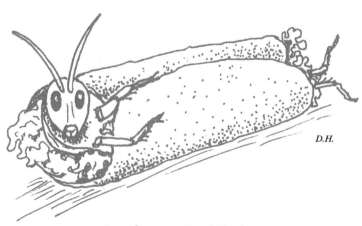

D.H.

Grasshopper Enchilada

Grasshopper Enchilada

1 tablespoon raisins
1 tablespoon chopped olives
1 tablespoon chopped almonds
Juice of 1 lemon
1 pound small grasshoppers,
    wings and hind legs removed
Salt and pepper to taste
15 tortillas
3 eggs, lightly beaten

1 medium jar seasoned
    tomato sauce
1/2 cup shredded Cheddar
    cheese
Chopped onion, shredded
    lettuce, tomatoes, sour
    cream, cheese and dry-
    roasted grasshoppers for
    garnish

Preheat oven to 350°. Mix raisins, olives, almonds, lemon juice, and grasshoppers; season with salt to taste. Soften tortillas on a griddle, dip in beaten egg, and fill with the grasshopper mixture. Roll up. Arrange seam side down in an ovenproof dish. Pour tomato sauce over and sprinkle with the cheese. Bake for 25–30 minutes, until heated through. Serves 6.

Special thanks to my friend Marta Ekola, a grade school science teacher who has served grasshopper cookies, cricket popcorn, and fried mealworms to her willing students. Nutritional information on insects and related recipes can be found on the Iowa State University website at http://www.ent.iastate.edu/Misc/InsectsAsFood.html. Be warned, the Department of Entomology at Iowa State University is not responsible for gastric distress, allergic reactions, feelings of repulsion, or other problems resulting from the ingestion of foods represented on their pages.

Other St. Urho's Day Recipes

If the thought of eating real bugs makes you queasy, you might want to serve a few of these "grasshopper" recipes instead. I promise, not a single hopper was harmed in the making of these dishes.

St. Urho's Grasshopper

1 part green crème de menthe	1 part Finlandia vodka
1 part white crème de cacao	Crushed ice

Pour all ingredients into a cocktail mixer; shake vigorously and strain into a chilled glass. Garnish with a green and white striped peppermint stick. Variation: If you are not fond of vodka, replace with an equal portion of light cream.

D.H.

Chocolate á la Mattson, traditionally known as a Flying Grasshopper

Chocolate á la Mattson

This drink, traditionally known as a Flying Grasshopper, was adapted by my brother Edwin Asala in honor of Sulo Havumaki who specified grasshoppers would replace frogs.

1/2 cup unsweetened cocoa
1/2 cup sugar
1/2 cup ice-cold water
1-1/2 teaspoons vanilla
Pinch of salt
1 cup cream
2-1/2 cups whole milk

1/2 cup crème de menthe
1 tablespoon crème de cacao
Whipping cream
Pinch of sugar
Chocolate shavings (optional)
Peppermint stick (optional)

Combine cocoa, sugar, water, vanilla and a pinch of salt in a large saucepan. Over low heat, whisk the ingredients to form a smooth paste. In a separate pot heat the cream and milk until just scalded. Slowly whisk into the cocoa mixture and simmer for 2 or 3 minutes. Blend in the crème de menthe and the crème de cacao. Carefully pour into individual mugs. Beat the cream and a pinch of sugar and top each of the mugs. If desired, sprinkle on chocolate shavings and add a peppermint stick. Serves 4.

Purple Haze

1 part Chambord
1 part vodka
Dash of sour mix

Cranberry juice to taste
Crushed ice

Combine all ingredients in a cocktail mixer; shake vigorously. Strain into shot glasses.

Purple Hooter

Here's a variation of the Purple Haze made with 7-Up.

1 part Chambord
1 part vodka
Dash of sour mix

Splash of 7-Up, or to taste
Crushed ice

Combine all ingredients in a cocktail mixer; shake vigorously. Strain into shot glasses.

St. Urho's Shake

Looking for a non-alcoholic drink to serve the kids? Try this yummy and healthy fruit smoothie.

1/2 cup unsweetened grape juice
1 cup milk

1 banana
Crushed ice

Blend all ingredients until smooth. Pour into tall glasses. Serves 2.

Purple Cow

Here's a fun variation of the more traditional Black Cow, and another non-alcoholic treat.

2 cups purple grape juice
1/2 cup milk
1 tablespoon sugar
1 teaspoon vanilla

1-1/2 cups vanilla ice cream
Ice cubes
Mint chocolate chip ice cream
   (optional)

Place grape juice, milk, sugar, vanilla and vanilla ice cream in blender. Top with enough ice cubes to fill the container. Blend until smooth. Top with a scoop of mint chocolate chip ice cream.

1 cup green grapes, sliced and seeded

1 cup purple grapes, sliced and seeded

1 cub cubed honeydew melon

1 cup diced Granny Smith apples

Romaine lettuce, shredded

Red leaf lettuce, shredded

For dressing:

1/4 cup olive oil

3 tablespoons lime juice

1-1/2 tablespoons wildflower honey

2 teaspoons fresh mint, minced fine

1/8 teaspoon dry mustard

Salt and pepper to taste

Combine grapes, honeydew and apples. Toss lightly with lettuce. Mix all dressing ingredients and serve alongside salad. Serves 4.

D.H.

Gooey Grasshopper Innards

1 (6-oz.) package butterscotch chips

6 cups prepared chow mein noodles, divided

2 cups lightly salted peanuts, divided

1 (6-oz.) package semi-sweet chocolate chips

In the top half of a double boiler, melt butterscotch chips, stirring constantly. Stir in 3 cups of the chow mein noodles and 1 cup of the peanuts. Drop by teaspoonfuls onto waxed paper and cool. Repeat procedure by melting the chocolate and combining with the remaining chow mein noodles and peanuts. Makes 60–80, enough for your child's classroom!

D.H.

Green Grasshopper Cake

Back in the 70s, I grew up across the street from my best friends Michelle and Christina. Their mother Olga made a terrific green cake she called Witch's Cake, and they all had me convinced that the green color came from grasshoppers that were mashed and added to the batter. I don't want to admit how old I really was before I learned the truth. . . .

1 (18-oz.) package white cake mix
3 small packages instant pistachio pudding and pie filling, divided
1-1/2 cups milk, divided
1/2 cup vegetable oil
1/2 cup cold water
5 eggs
1/2 cup chopped pistachio nuts*
1 cup heavy cream
Few drops green food coloring
1 cup sweetened flake coconut

Preheat oven to 350°. Grease and flour two 9-inch round cake pans. In a large bowl, combine the cake mix, 2 packages of the instant pudding and pie filling, 1/2 cup milk, and the oil and water. Beat until smooth. Beat in the eggs one at a time until batter is smooth. Fold in nuts. Pour into the cake pans and bake for 30 minutes or until a toothpick inserted in the center comes out clean.

Cool cakes for at least 20 minutes before removing from the pans, then turn out and cool completely. To make the frosting, beat the heavy cream together with the remaining milk and the third package of pudding mix. Add a few drops of food coloring to enhance the color. Frost the cake with this mixture. Sprinkle the top and sides with the coconut. Serves 12.

I know, I promised there would be no real grasshoppers in this section of recipes, but if you want to replace the chopped pistachio nuts with crushed, oven-dried grasshoppers, I certainly won't stop you.

Grasshopper Cream Pie

Here is another "grasshopper" dessert straight from my childhood. You can replace the chocolate wafers with Oreo cookies.

18 chocolate wafer cookies, pulverized
4 tablespoons butter
3/4 cup whole milk, heated to just below boiling
2 dozen large puffy marshmallows
1/4 cup crème de menthe
2 tablespoons white crème de cacao
Green food coloring (optional)
1 cup heavy cream, whipped
Chocolate shavings, whipped cream for garnish

Combine chocolate wafers with butter and press into the bottom and sides of a 9-inch pie dish to form a crust. Refrigerate at least one hour. In a large saucepan, melt marshmallows in the milk. Remove; set aside to cool. Add crème de menthe, crème de cacao and food coloring if desired. Fold in whipped cream. Pour into pie shell and freeze. Slice; sprinkle with chocolate shavings and top with whipped cream before serving.

D.H.

Hungry Hoppers

Grasshoppers sailing for North America

Kuopio, Finland, sister city of Minneapolis, Minnesota, has been celebrating St. Urho's Day since 1981. In the spirit of the day, the following telegram was received by the Minneapolis celebrants:

> *"Se on taas se Pyhan Urhon Paiva*
> *Kuopion Kaupunginhallitus toivottaa 16.3 joohdosta*
> *memestyst kaikille ystavyyskaupunkimme Minneapoliksen*
> *Suomalaisille samoin kuin suomalaisille merelta merelle*
> *'Rapakon takana'"*
> *Kuopion Kaupunginhallitus*
> *Juhani Koskinen   Heikki Viitala*

Songs of the Season

What's a holiday without music? One night, after a few too many grasshopper drinks, my mother and I sat down to write a couple of songs for St. Urho's Day. Next March, as the rest of the world is singing the praises of an Irish saint, sing these songs instead and take pride in your Finnish heritage. Sing them loud, sing them proud!

"Toons" by Donna and Joanne

Oh, St. Urho
(To the tune of "Danny Boy")

Oh, St. Urho, the hoppers, the hoppers are singing.
From field to field, and throughout the countryside.
The grapes are ripe, and ready for picking.
'Tis you, 'tis you
Who must chase the hoppers away.
But come they back, tomorrow or next season,
To eat our pur-ple grapes once again.
Then you'll be here to chase them from fair Finland.
Oh St. Urho boy, Oh St. Urho boy,
We need you so.

Fertile Fields of Finland
(To the tune of "America the Beautiful")

It's harvest time, the fields are green
As far as I can see!
The purple grapes, so ripe and sweet,
Will make the finest wine!
Saint Urho, oh! Saint Urho, oh!
To you we give our thanks.
If not for you, we know it's true,
There'd be grasshoppers in our ranks.

Battle Hymn of St. Urho
(To the tune of "Battle Hymn of the Republic")

Mine eyes have seen the hoppers
By the dozen and the score.
They are chomping on our vintage
Where our grape crop has grown.
But our Finnish boy, St. Urho,
Will chase them all away
With careful-ly chosen words.
Glory! Glory! Hallelujah!
Glory! Glory! It's St. Urho!
Glory! Glory! Hallelujah!
St. Urho will save the day!

D.H.

What Shall We Do with the Hoppers, Urho?
(To the tune of "Drunken Sailor")
We've provided a few verses, I'm sure you can come up with many more on your own!

Chorus:
What shall we do with the hoppers, Urho?
What shall we do with the hoppers, Urho?
What shall we do with the hoppers, Urho?
Now that we've got them?

Grind them up for fertilizer (3 times),
For next year's crops.

Chorus

Dip them in chocolate, one by one, (3 times)
They make a tasty treat.

Chorus

It's a Long Way from Finland
(To the tune of "It's a Long Way to Tipperary")

It's a long way from our dear Finland
It's a long way we go.
It's a long way from our dear Finland
Urho said we had to go.
Good bye, ready harvest!
Farewell, grapes so keen!
It's a long, long way from our dear Finland,
But my stomach's still there!

A Bunch of Grapes
(To the tune of "All Around My Hat")

All around my hat,
I'll wear a bunch of purple grapes, oh.
All around my hat,
For a year and a day,
And if anyone should ask me
The reason why I'm wearing them,
It's all for St. Urho, the boy
Who chased the hoppers away.

D.H.

A Finnish Lullaby
(To the tune of "An Irish Lullaby" or "Too Ra Loo Ra Looral")

It was up in Minnesota
Many years ago
My *äiti* (mother) sang a song to me,
About her friend Urho.
Just a simple little ditty,
Of the boy who saved the day.
How we should all give thanks because
He chased the hoppers away.

Chorus:

Urho, my dear Urho,
Urho, my dear Urho,
Urho, my dear Urho,
Hush now, don't you cry!
Urho, my dear Urho,
Urho, my dear Urho,
Urho, my dear Urho,
That's a Finnish lullaby!

D.H.

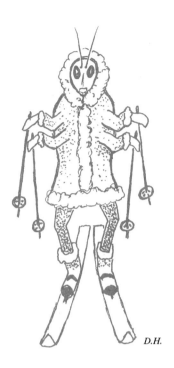

Hopper on skis leaving Finland.

"Toons" by Janice Laulainen

Urho Sase the Hoppers Out
(To the tune of "Michael Row Your Boat Ashore")

Urho sase the hoppers out, hallelujah.
Urho sase the hoppers out, hallelujah.
Urho is the poy for me, hallelujah.
Urho is the poy for me, hallelujah.
The Finland fjords are chilly and cold, hallelujah.
Freese tose krasshoppers little toes, hallelujah.
The Finland fjords are deep and vide, hallelujah
Hoppers are swimming for the other side, hallelujah.

Home on the Iron Range
(To the tune of "Home on the Range")

Oh give me a home, where grasshoppers roam,
Where Finns ride them around all day.
When grapes turn to wine,
And Finns have a good time
And have a grasshopper feast at suppertime.

Grasshopper Swarms
(To the tune of "When Irish Eyes are Smiling")

The grasshoppers swarmed over Finland
And destroyed the vineyard crop.
St. Urho came to the rescue,
Murmured words to make them stop.
Now Finland has no grasshoppers
As you can plainly see.
Give our thanks to St. Urho
Who helped to set her free.

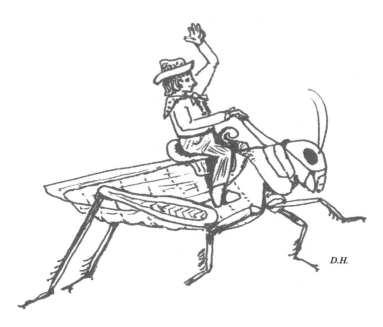

D.H.

St. Urho's Day Parade
by Eino Amous

The original of this song, inscribed in Runic letters, was found on an old Finnish flatbread board, lodged under the water in Blueberry River. By the time that it was deciphered by Professor Viisamaki, Helsinki, the board had crumbled from exposure to air. *

St. Urho's Day Parade
(To the tune of Burl Ives' "Killigrew's Soiree")

There were Ahos, Altos, Basos and Kallios,
Puljus, Bousu's and Hallikainens, too.
Karjalas and Rajalas and flatbread homemade
All dressed in green and purple for St. Urho's Day Parade.

There were Erkkilas, Sarkelas, Beldos and Haatajas,
Seppalas and Hepolas and Hepokoskis, too.
Kinnunens and Sakkinens and knitted socks homemade,
All dressed in green and purple for St. Urho's Day Parade.

There were Jarvis, Sarvis, Marjamaas and Lallis,
Makis and Koskis and Koskiniemis, too.
Mattilas and Markulas and *mojakka* homemade,
All dressed in green and purple for St. Urho's Day Parade.

There were Saaris, Saimis, Saukkos and Alajokis,
Peralas and Pesolas and Keskitalos, too.
Ruonas and Ranuas and *viiliä* homemade.
All dressed in green and purple for St. Urho's Day Parade.

* *Editor's note: Editor David Torrel says the name of the author and the professor are obviously spoofs. We have searched everywhere, including the missing person's area of the Internet, in vain to find the true author of this poem, who is apparently buried in the folklore archives of the people. Georgia Heald, one of our editors, suggests that "Eino Amous" is related to "A. Nonymous," who she thinks was a Brit.*

St. Urho Polka
By Lloyd Houle and The Norshor Neighbors
Sponsored by Finland Recreation Area Committee

To quote from Norshor Records "This is a fun song that was made up while we were working on Roy Johnson's grasshopper float in 1977."

Poor old St. Urho
He is so tired
Chasing the hoppers away.
Poor old St. Urho
He isn't dancing
He is too tired to play.
Give him a sauna!
Give him a *lempi* (love)!
Give him a *tytto* (girl) so fair.
Then he'll be dancing
And be romancing
Have not another care.
There goes St. Urho
He is so happy

Now he has time to play.
Dance around St. Urho
Have fun St. Urho
For you have saved the day.
All singing phrases
Within his praises
Suomalainen poika (Finnish boy)
You are.
We salute you
Sing tributes to you
You are the greatest by far!

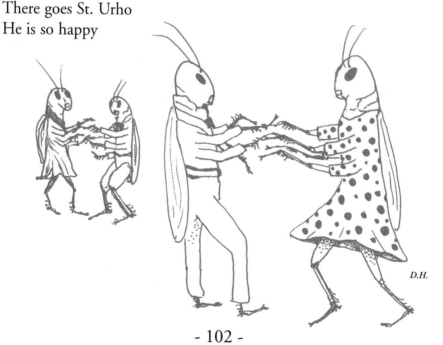

D.H.

St. Urho Story Singers

David Torrel's "Ode to St. Urho" and the "Ballad of St. Urho" found on the following pages is in the tradition of a people preserving the lore and legend of their time.

Minnesota high school teachers, Torrel of Sparta and Mark Eskola of Duluth, musican and arranger, with others recorded many songs for fans of the saint. Radio stations have featured them on the Saint's day.

In writing their St. Urho poems and lyrics, Finnish Americans continue the tradition of their folk epic, *The Kalevala*, which was collected as oral poetry and published in written form by Elias Lönnrot on February 28, 1835. Kalevala Day is still celebrated each year on February 28.

Photo by Darlene Niska

Ready for St. Urho's Day, David Torrel of Sparta, Minnesota, wears his grasshopper hat and purple shirt.

The singing or writing of verse tells of a people and the world of their time.

Of note also is the children's book, A Tale for St. Urho's Tay, *by Aini Rajanen. Now out-of-print, it featured St. Urho with color illustrations.*

Ode to St. Urho
by David Torrel, with producer, arranger Mark Eskola

The time has come to talk of great things
of soldiers and wars and kings.
Of deeds so great and mighty and bold
of battles fought and won in time of old.
Where the good have strived and beaten the foe,
and the greatest is the Finnish St. Urho!
The country of Finland was beset by plagues
of grasshoppers that came in raids.
They ate all the corn and the wheat and the grapes.
They covered the fields and the roads and the lakes.
Chase them out! Chase them out!
Chase them out! Chase them out!
The noble and the good St. Urho.
'Twas then that Urho came upon the scene
to do battle with the mob of pests.
His back was wet with honest sweat,
the hoppers moved out with his big threat.
Chase them out! Chase them out!
Chase them out! Chase them out!
The noble and the good St. Urho.
The tears did go, the joy returned,
the people did fear no more.
St. Urho has chased the grasshoppers out,
the damaged land once again did sprout.
They are out! They are out!
They are out! They are out!
Because of the good St. Urho.
So here's to him the good St. Urho,
for his fight against the foe.
He was not well known when the war began,
but then became a real fighting man.
He has fought and strived and beaten the foe,
Ho tay and cheers for good ol' St. Urho!

Ballad of St. Urho
by David Torrel, with producer, arranger Mark Eskola
"The Ode" and "The Ballad" are available on cassette.

Whenever you talk about the brave men of old
    and all of their honour that you've been told.
Be sure that you mention the Finn named Urho
    and tell of his greatness to all young and old.
Some men are born great and some men achieve it
    but Urho himself never would believe it.

Urho was born on a farm in Finland,
    raised on bread and milk and stew till he was four.
The grasshoppers came and they ate all his *mojakka*,
    got him so mad that he kicked on the floor.
He ran in the field and he stamped and cussed.
The grasshoppers turned his hay fields into dust.

As he grew older, he disliked those hoppers,
    he never forgot what they had done before.
As the years went on, he developed some tactics,
    he knew that someday he would settle the score.
The hoppers grew bigger and longer and tougher,
    Urho had to act or his people would suffer.

Starting to clear them from one end of Finland,
    never stopping till the hoppers were gone.
Others had quit and had gone home to rest,
    they are glad that Urho got rid of that pest.
Urho had to come and the hoppers had to go,
    it was nice when they had the good St. Urho.

St. Urho Lives in Cyberspace
by Joan Liffring-Zug Bourret

Just type "St. Urho" in an Internet search, and you will find a number of interesting sites. Of note is one about the saint and Menahga, Minnesota. A video is offered of the Menahga St. Urho celebration, mostly in English. The site lists celebrations of St. Urho in Minnesota at Finland, Squaw Lake, Virginia, Fairbault, and Duluth; at Butte, Montana; several places in Oregon, Idaho, and Michigan, and on college campuses. Evidently, a new Vermont Chapter of St. Urho faithfuls has been spawned. The University of Toronto now celebrates the March 16 saint's day. Also, it notes that the "*mojakka*" feast was "truly superb." The site-masters joke that the **real (?)** Finnish President Tarja Halonen actually came within 180 miles of being sworn in as the new Mayor of Menahga.

The text inscribed at the base of the St. Urho statue by Bemidji State College professor Sulo Havumaki is included on the screen.

Another home page shows the Helsinki Boulevard sign in Menahga, as well as a sign with this message:

Welcome to the home of St. Urho.
Gateway to the pines.
Finest sand beach in Minnesota.

Elsewhere, you will find that Petrus Kaartinen, a Finnish student, discovered St. Urho ten years ago and has become "St. Urho's Finnish Ambassador."

Other links show the statue of St. Urho listed as a roadside attraction along with other oddities such as the Kensington Runestone at Alexandria, Minnesota, and Belle Plaine's two-story outhouse. The compiler of this list shows the grasshopper carried on the pitchfork of the Menahga fiberglass St. Urho statue, as well as the head of the Finland, Minnesota statue of St. Urho. An editorial note says the ten-foot sculpture across the street, of a fish holding a beer keg, is preferable to the Saint.

You can even order St. Urho greeting cards from a site on the web.
It's all in the eye of the beholder. St. Urho joins Elvis in living on
with a growing number of sites, and "sightings."

A Final Word
by Bob Kaari

The town of Menahga, Minnesota is host to one of the two known statues of St. Urho. In commemoration of the saint, the local paper, Review Messenger, *published a booklet called "The History of St. Urho." The following story tells the* **true** *history of St. Urho. Reprinted with permission.*

I was sitting at the typewriter early this week, putting together a story on St. Urho, the cleric revered by all us true sons of Finland for his freeing the homeland from grasshoppers, when my cousin Arvo stormed into the office, dropped his chain saw on the floor and growled: "Ay spose yew gon' write summa dat domb stuff ëpout Sant Urho shase ta krasshoppers oudda Finland, hah?"

I said, yes, I was writing a story about St. Urho, so what?

"Vall," said Arvo, shifting his snoose. "Dey tal ta story wrong. Dey gotta whole ting scroon up. Ferda cripesakes, dey ain' effen gotta hiss name spoke ridte. Dey call him Ear Ho! Ear Ho fer da cripesakes. His name is Oor Ho. Goota go ërounna toungue witta Oor."

I allowed that some foreign influence had crept into the language due to recent immigration.

"Yah," said Arvo, "All dem foreigners . . . da Arish, da Tgermans, da Svedes, da Bonhonk . . . hardly enny Amarkans lef'. Dey gotta story all scroonup, too," he added.

"How's that?" I asked.

Arvo said he heard the true story of St. Urho from his grandfather, Waino, who was "hummert per cent fer da troot, like tat odder great Finlander — Amarakan Georg Washingtinen."

"Georg Washingtinen?"

"Yah, yew know ta guy vat with ta Revelloshin . . . he war with Toma Jeffersinen an' Ban Frankolinen."

"Oh, yeah, now I know."

Arvo said his grandfather, who always told the truth, said that the ancient legend about St. Urho chanting *"Heinäsirkka, heinäsirkka, mene täältä hiiteen!"* was pure fiction.

In the first place, Grandfather Waino pointed out, the nation in those days was called Vinland. This was because it was a great grape-growing nation, even exporting grape juice to Italy. But then, the grasshoppers came.

Waino said the destruction to the vineyards was horrible. The rapacious green pests stripped the leaves from the vines, even chewed off the stems. Only a few gallons of grape juice had been saved and these were stored in an old stone building. By March 16, 1643 or was it 1644? the frightened peasants marched to the Helsinki Monastery to plead with the wisest and most beloved exponent of *sisu*, Brother Urho, to save the grapes.

Brother Urho strode through the depleted vineyards, tears rolling down his face as he viewed the disaster. In a fit of anger, he grabbed a handful of grasshoppers and hurled them into the sea, and was astonished to see a huge salmon rise up and swallow them. Quickly he threw another handful into the water and the scene was repeated.

Rushing back to the monastery, Brother Urho grabbed his fish-pole and returned to the seaside where he shouted the famous words: *"Heinäsirkka, heinäsirkka, sinä menet kalastamaan,"* which means "Grasshopper, grasshopper, you are going fishing!"

Whereupon he flipped the bait into the sea and was immediately fast to a trophy salmon. A great cry went up from the peasants who all ran home and returned with their fishing tackle to start hauling in salmon. In a very short time the vineyards had all been cleaned of grasshoppers for fish bait. And there was a great feasting of fish, so much so that the nation changed its name from Vinland to Finland.

Urho, of course, was later elevated to sainthood for discovering that grasshoppers were excellent fish bait . . . and incidentally saving the vineyards. Grandfather Waino pointed out, as a sidelight, that in the rush to catch salmon, the people had forgotten about the small amount of grape juice that had been set aside, which in due course fermented. But the story of how the Finlanders invented wine would be for another time, Arvo assured me.

"An dat," Arvo concluded, "iss da troot about Sant Urho, fer da cripesakes."

D.H.

Hopper bait on a fishhook

Books by Mail

Finnish-American Folklore: by Joanne Asala
    The Legend of St. Urho (this book) $12.95
FinnFun by Bernhard Hillila $12.95
Suomi Specialities by Sinikka Grönberg Garcia $12.95
    Finnish Celebrations, Recipes and Traditions
Finnish Proverbs by Inkeri Väänänen-Jensen $10.95
Words of Magic and Wisdom from The Kalevala
    by Richard Impola $12.95
Finnish Short Stories $18.95
    Revised and Expanded
Fine Finnish Foods by Gerry Kangas $6.95
Fantastically Finnish: Recipes and Traditions $9.95
Complete catalog of all titles: $2.50

Shipping: $4.95 for orders under $25.00. Over $25, add $5.95. Over $75, add $7.95.

Please send orders to:
Penfield Press
215 Brown Street
Iowa City, Iowa 52245

Penfield Press titles in the Penfield Press web store are easily found on the Internet under Finnish titles. Enter Penfield.